FEAR, PHOBIAS *and* FREEDOM

Discovering the Key to Living Fearlessly Free

DAN BROOKS

BALBOA.
PRESS
A DIVISION OF HAY HOUSE

Balboa Press books may be ordered through booksellers or by contacting:

Balboa Press
A Division of Hay House
1663 Liberty Drive
Bloomington, IN 47403
www.balboapress.com
1-(877) 407-4847

ISBN: 978-1-4525-6005-2 (sc)
ISBN: 978-1-4525-6007-6 (hc)
ISBN: 978-1-4525-6006-9 (e)

Library of Congress Control Number: 2012918392

Printed in the United States of America

Balboa Press rev. date: 10/08/2012

"Fear is the Wall which keeps us from seeing our True Potential"

—*Dan Brooks*

The Promised Intention

I promised myself I would live this life in wondrous experience.

I would remember my spiritual evolution.

I would awaken the power inside of me.

I would see that all paths taken have led me to this very point.

I would realize my gift and I would share it with others.

I would truly understand 'The Pursuit of Happiness'.

I would see the beauty and the adversity and recognize the contrast.

I would realize the wondrous beauty in the contrast.

I would find the seed of hope in all adversity.

I would inspire thousands to find their inner peace.

I would find myself through the experiences of others.

I would learn what Love truly is

And,

I would live my life without fear.

Dan Brooks

CONTENTS

THE COVER ART STORY

When I asked my son Nicholas, who is an amazing artist, to paint a picture of fear based beliefs, I knew he would create a work of art. He has an amazing ability to capture the essence of an idea and create his art as he has done for me so many times before. I feel his art can be interpreted by acknowledging the details within each picture, but below are the words he has used to describe the emotions and flow of this artful experience.

"There can be a number of things standing between you and your goals. When my dad asked me to create something that represented overcoming fears I wanted to say as much with the picture as I could. So rather than depicting fear as some scary image I chose the symbol for an electrical resistor. This opens up the door to a number of other useful interpretations as well. For example, a resistor may not necessarily prevent the path from being achieved but it can significantly slow the progress. I think the most important part of the message to get across is that whatever happens to be standing between you and your desires; be it a deep seeded phobia or a lack of knowledge as to how to achieve your goal, you have the power to overcome that obstacle. It's never too late to break out of old habits and challenge yourself to seek your desires. Sometimes, the way we think about things is operating on a level so deep that without resolving internal conflicts we may be setting ourselves up for failure, and so changing the way we think in order to benefit our lives and/ or the lives of those around us can range from something simple to something that may take a bit more work.

The symbols along the upper part of the picture are assumed to represent goals, but some of them are faded as if to suggest that too much resistance stands between it and the individual. We can also think of these goals/achievements as something the individual may not even be considering as a potential pathway. When you consider what you want out of life, it may be that an experience or form of knowledge that has not yet crossed your path has the potential to create an entirely new set of desires within you. Our world is filled with endless possibilities as to what we can do and be. The cutting edge of innovative thought can be both terrifying and exhilarating. Will you courageously follow your desires? Explore the possibilities that you may not yet even know about?"

Nicholas *(Tatsujinsan)* Brooks

YouTube channel: www.youtube.com/tatsujinsan

Website: www.tatsujinsan.moonfruit.com

Fear is neither good nor bad.

It can be a wall we think is too high to get beyond or it can let us know we are not quite ready to receive what we want.

Either way, when conquered, we realize it was merely a hurdle we only had to cross to find happiness

—Dan Brooks

PROLOGUE

Last night as I sat in my front room I watched as the flashes of light from an approaching thunderstorm became brighter and brighter. The storm was nearly upon our small community. The skies rumbled and the wind picked up with each moment that passed. What started off to be a little light show was very soon turning into a wicked storm.

The flashes lit up the darkness in my yard and the loud cracks of thunder followed closer and closer. Within a couple of minutes the bursts of thunder were so loud it would shake the dishes in the china cabinet. The forest around my home became very quiet with the exception of the wind and one bird pleasantly chirping away.

I stood in complete awe as I looked out my window and I was completely fascinated by the power of which nature was unleashing on us. Thunderstorms are one of those natural things I have always been excited to watch. Flash . . . BOOM!, and again Flash . . . BOOM! What a marvelous light show nature was putting on before me.

And then, I looked at my dog and there she was cowering on the couch shaking in complete fear of what was happening. She was never like this as a puppy as she and I would sit in front of the window when a storm came along and enjoy the show together. I wondered what had changed in her to make her so fearful of something which never mattered before.

"There, there, Piddles. It's only a storm. Why are you so afraid?", I asked her. Of course she could not answer but I could not calm her down either.

I wondered if this was what early mankind was like long time ago when, because of some emotional event or new found belief, we perceived something we did not understand as a fearful event. I wondered if this unexplainable and dreadful Fear we were experiencing had us cowering in caves or huddled under trees.

How did we express this fear to our tribesmen?

It must have been a catastrophic event indeed without any knowledge of what was happening. Surely it must have felt like the sky was angry with us for something we may have done. Maybe if we performed a ritual of sorts the sky would quit being angry with us. So we performed some sort of chant or ritual and low-and-behold the sky quit shouting out it's angry thunderous crashes and the winds subsided.

"This must be the answer", we cried out. "Perform this ritual and the sky/Gods will no longer be angry with us."

We spread the word to other tribesman, some who had never feared the angry sky before, and they began to perform their rituals so that they too would be free of the fear of harm.

Today we understand this beautiful phenomenon as something completely different. We can comprehend that the Gods are not angry with us. It is merely a natural event that happens from time to time and is only a sign of a storm coming in.

We understand the event so for many people they do not fear what they understand. And yet . . . There are so many people, despite the knowledge who still cower in fear at a natural event like this.

There are nearly 1800 thunderstorms per day on our planet or 1.4 billion lightning strikes per year. You stand a better chance of winning the lottery than you do at getting hit by lightning.

Knowledge and understanding always replaces Fear.

Fear, Phobias and FREEDOM

Discovering the Key to living Fearlessly free!

We will never find peace within ourselves until we free ourselves from Fear. When we are free of Fear we can no longer be controlled by our own victimization and those who repress the truly creative, loving and compassionate beings that we are.

—*Dan Brooks*

INTRODUCTION

I have come to realize that we all have a unique gift. It is not a gift of super powers, psychic abilities or extra sensory perception. Although that may be the case with some people it is not for the majority.

We spend so much time trying to figure our life out that often times we miss the very thing that prevents us from enjoying it to its fullest.

Isn't Happiness what we are all looking for?

We want to have the perfect relationship, the perfect house, the perfect life and we feel it is in the possession of having these things where we will finally be happy.

The longer we spend brooding over 'Why' everyone else is getting their fair share and we are not, only takes us further from finding this very simple gift that we have. It is in the discovery of our 'Is-ness' where all our power lies. It is not vague or generalized in its nature but instead a definiteness of purpose. A refined jewel that is sealed within us all and the discovery of it unlocks the very intention of why you came to this physical plain to experience life, love, joy and happiness.

The key to discovering our unique gift is in beginning to understand that everything we have been told up to this very point in life is from someone else's perception and not that of our own discovery.

The doorway to getting what we want is in letting go of our Fears and changing our perception of our very own emotional events that have made us who we are. Realizing that all of our experiences right to this very moment have been laid out in such a way that we can use every heartache and every sorrow as the foundation of becoming that person we dream of becoming.

There is a discovery within ourselves of overcoming our Fear and understanding our world around us just a little more.

It is not in the wanting of more that brings us happiness but instead the appreciation of what we have and who we are that opens life up to us.

"When you let go of trying to get more of what you really don't need, it frees up oceans of energy to make a difference with what you already have"—Lynne Twist

This is an amazing time to experience life. The internet has provided us with the means to discover more three dimensional thinking to look at the challenges we currently face from all angles and then decide for ourselves which path feels right to us. Not just a two dimensional, black & white version of what we have been led to believe by the keepers of knowledge. LIFE is in full color.

Never before in our time have we ever had the ability to reverse all diseases, embark on new sources of renewable energy and holistically heal every aspect of our life from emotional, spiritual and physical challenges. In the 'old' way of fearful thinking we are limited and defective, but those days are coming to a close and we have the opportunity to see this physical life journey as it truly stands one of compassion, love and forgiveness.

In this book you will be taken on a journey of discovery, realization and solutions to repair every aspect of your life. You will be given the 'Formula for Success' and happiness, I guarantee you will.

I have never had the ability to solve riddles and to me, life is not a riddle, it is simplistic in nature and all the answers lie within each and every one of us. The important thing to note here is that all resolutions are simplistic in nature. Life challenges were never meant to be difficult to figure out; we were not meant to suffer. The only thing that makes us suffer through a life challenge is our inability to open our minds and hearts to a new form of thinking outside our current beliefs.

Napoleon Hill said it best "All great truths are simple in final analysis and easily understood; if they are not, they are not great truths"

I feel blessed I was brought up in a home where I was encouraged to think independently outside the dogma which was being given to me by religion, schools, healthcare and government. It was not because my parents were free-thinkers; they were just older than most parents of my peers and really didn't want to be bothered explaining things to an inquisitive child. I do not say this to give the impression that my parents were bad parents by any means; I could not have been born to a more perfect couple. My mother and father were in their 40's by the time I was born and I was the last of three children. They had led full lives and had faced many adversities and challenges both physical and emotionally by this time.

From a very young age I saw things differently than most people. It challenged my parents who were set in their ways and beliefs when it came to doing most things and my inquisitive mind was told to "Do as I Say." This got me into some interesting disagreements with my parents which I would never win and usually ended up with some sort of punishment or conclusive statement like "That's the way it is, so there, period!".

My childhood was however, 'free-form' thinking and my curiousness towards believing that things were not always as they appear set me on a life path which I would not discover the meaning of until years later.

Because of free-form thinking I found it challenging to buy into many of the dogmas which were being taught. 'Things' according to the system, just didn't make sense to me, they did not Feel right. When I challenged those ideologies the authority figure would punish me, but I could not stop challenging conventional thinking. School and church in the early 1960's taught many topics that I could not quite wrap my mind around from the explanation of gravity, dinosaurs, democracy, the atom bomb, Adam & Eve, and most subjects actually, especially within the dogma of religion. There were far too many hypocrisies and unexplainable story guidelines to just knowingly surrender to that linear thinking.

"Teacher, why is the sky Blue? Because, if it was Green we wouldn't know when to stop mowing our lawns, so there, period".

I didn't stand a snowballs chance in Hell against the linear thinking of adults. In the long run, they won out because who was I, as this young person, to challenge 'Beliefs" laid down over hundreds of years. Of course the fear induced in me from the fear of punishment helped me to conform.

When I lost my father at the age of 13, I was left with even more time to think and feel for myself which created even more curiosity and denial within me. For a while I felt alone and hated that 'God' had taken my father who I loved so much away from me. Looking back now I can see how the seeds of bitterness and emptiness grew inside of me. Life became very serious and a lot less fun now because I was expected to be the man of the house and help my mother run a business while, it seemed, the whole world was out playing and having fun.

Could this beautiful planet we live on really be as bad and as structured as I was led to believe?

I noticed there was a reaction to every action, but according to society the reactions were usually painful in either an emotional or physical punishment of some sort for non-conformity. It seems now that I chose the painful way of trying to figure things out because there was always a repercussive effect to every decision I made. The interesting thing is that it never completely killed my spirit of always asking 'Why', 'What' or 'How'. I still felt there had to be an easier way of doing things and resolving challenges.

Right out of school and into the workplace I discovered I had a unique ability to 'fix' things which were broken or not working right. Applying this to machines appeared to be the logical path for me. Even in industry we were taught to fix and not look at the cause of the problem. Here though, in this working world, I could explore and experiment with my reasoning of finding causal solutions to problems and it worked.

I developed the ability to break problems down and compartmentalize them to find the solution to the real 'Cause' of the problem. I was allowed to invent and re-engineer machines for more reliable and efficient production. Even assembly procedures could be refined to make them more efficient and productive. I was saving companies hundreds of thousands of dollars annually with my ideas and for the first time in my life I felt free to think and discover and use my senses to diagnose and fix things.

By the age of 21 I was at the top of my field and companies were paying head-hunters to coerce me to work for them. Winning awards and bonuses for outstanding work were commonplace.

This is where I need you to understand I was no genius and did not possess any other skill than the ability to ask the question 'Why' and be persistent in finding a solution. In most cases it was just a 'gut feeling' that something wasn't right and it could be improved on.

Over the many years of my working life I have been blessed to work in many industries and with many remarkable teachers. When I was asking the question 'Why' and presenting solutions I was happiest. When this process was not validated in my job, my life would unravel and I would become depressed. It is clear to me now, this is why I could not remain with a company for any more than a couple of years. The challenge was gone or the machine [company] would be working efficiently OR, the powers-that-be were not open to change.

The feeling of the old ideology and linear thinking would simply chase me away. The interesting thing was, it would chase me into the darker corners of my mind where all the 'stuff' I had been conforming to was residing and I would become very unhappy and depressed once again.

The Darker Moments turn into the Darker Years;

Within all of us, lie those emotional events where we made decisions which did not give us positive results. We have all done things which we regret afterward and it seems the longer we are on this earth we build a cache of those events which can tear down the very structure of our belief in ourselves. That place where we fail to see the beauty and wonderment of life and we travel on the road of turmoil and confusion. We fail to see our own uniqueness and succumb to our inner fears of inadequacy.

It begins with one event as a child trying to find our way in a physical world we do not understand and then it appears that it just keeps building. We chalk these things up as failures when in actuality they are our life lessons, our experience of all things. This can be the point where our most inner fears take over and yet there is only one fear; the fear of failing itself. "If I do this, then that is going to happen again so why bother trying".

In reality, these challenges are the contrast and the fuel we are searching for to make us become more.

It is not life that has changed, there were always challenges it was my emotional compass that would change. What I had focused on became skewed and led me back into the darkness of my own consciousness and my inability to focus on what really should matter, life, love, family, friends and happiness.

The longer I would remain in this darkness the more I would fear the ability to change. I had become a product of my darkest thoughts and saw no hope and no light.

Somewhere along the way, my thinking changed. In my early forties I can remember a particular event that caused a major shift in my thinking. It was when I awoke one morning and swung my swollen arthritic feet out of bed. The arthritis was so bad in my body it caused me a great deal of pain to put weight on my feet. My body ached all over and as I walked past the full length mirror I saw an image of a man I had not seen in a very long time, it was my fathers' reflection as my own. I was bent over from the pain of life weighted on my shoulders and the essence of my spirit gone from my eyes leaving only a dullness which would reflect back at me.

My father led an extremely rough life from early childhood during the Great Depression', through a world war and then surgery after surgery from a crush injury he received while working as a lumberjack for the forestry companies. He looked like he was 70 years old when he was 50.

As I stood there looking at this image of me as this old crippled man I thought that my life was coming to a close. I remember saying to myself, "Well, Brooksy you've 5 years left in you if you are lucky before death finds you." All I could see was my life ending. I was looking to see the worst in myself instead of the best in myself. It really didn't matter because I was in the place of self-doubt and loathing and on a path of self-destruction.

Seeing this image changed me in some way, was I truly at life's crossroads or was there something more for me. Something changed in me, it began with one small realization around health. One small change that made me start asking the question 'Why' again and I began to discover that health, wealth and happiness are all tied together in one thing and that thing is our gift of emotional freedom.

The one small thing I began doing was taking vitamins and supplements. It was through a direct sales company and part of becoming an active distributor was my first exposure to personal development.

Up to this point in my life I was like 99.9% of the rest of the population of earth, thinking and believing I was alone in my thinking. All these fears and self-doubts had rooted themselves very deeply in my psyche and I believed if I could not think my way out of this there would only be a life of mediocrity at best which would be filled with pain and early death just as my father had suffered.

Those barriers were about to be challenged and the old me was in the early process of being revealed again. After only a few months of taking supplements I had lost a lot of weight, my pain began to subside and I started questioning my current habits. I began asking 'Why' this worked so well for me. If these supplements work what else can bring me out of this painful existence. And so the new journey down a new path spread out before me.

Soon personal development books made their way into my library and the knowledge I gleaned from them refueled the lost curiosity I had left behind so long ago. I found this new way of thinking laid out in these books to be colorful and three dimensional. I began to feel again. I don't mean feel like the way TV portrays Love or the way society tells us we must feel towards others. What I felt was my inner intuition kicking in and asking for more research more answers, new perspectives on the old ideals of health.

In my younger days I can remember asking my parents if they thought there would ever be a cure for all diseases and if suffering could ever be resolved. They assured me we were only a few years away from man (doctors) discovering all the inner secrets of the body and curing diseases with just one pill. I realize now how completely UN-true this perception was. Not by the fault of my parents, but by our naivety that government, media and doctors would not lie to us and were there to protect the human race. Little did I realize then that those very same powers bear the largest blame in our 'social fear'!

When I discovered new healing modalities I began to research them all to see what was working and what was not working. I discovered many things which were no better than a placebo effect. Then I discovered how <u>powerful</u> the placebo effect was and how it worked in 1/3 of all healing of the body.

I began to ask 'Why' again. If the placebo effect is so powerful then it must be the mind/body experience that heals not the treatment. This has led me to this one conclusion . . . *There is no such thing as a Miracle cure, the miracle of creating the cure lies within each and every one of us.*

It is not genetic, we are not defective, and it is our state of mind that begins the healing process and our intuition that guides us to the correct remedy answers. True healing, or what I call FREEDOM, comes in overcoming our fears and self proclaimed limitations and false perceptions of how things work in this universe.

Freedom can mean many things to many people. Some believe that financial freedom is what will make them happy. Others believe finding there soul mate is the freedom they seek to find happiness. I will tell you this there is but one freedom and that my friend is the freedom we get when we conquer our fears and realize our gift of love and compassion towards the whole of humanity that we have all been blessed with. It is our true perfection but we could not get to the light without experiencing the darkness within ourselves. But know this, there are shortcuts we can take, there are tools we can use to move ourselves from these programmed feeble beings we have become to realize our connection to the most powerful force in the universe. That is who you truly are.

My gift was a plain as the nose on my face and I never really thought about much until I was asked what my life 'Purpose' was. After years of contemplating and cursing this question I realized My gift in its simplicity is I love to fix broken 'things' and I do this with this one thought in mind . . . "I ask Why is it broken".

Finding ways to help fix broken Human beings is the greatest challenge of all. The complexity of this amazing body we live in intertwined with the energy field that is connected to all things creates the woven pattern of life itself. Perhaps there are no solutions or perhaps the solutions are as simple as finding inner peace and growth.

The journey you are about to begin can be complex in its explanation and yet so simple when you comprehend the information and the power of the tools I will share with you.

The Opinions, hypotheses, and beliefs expressed in this book are from my experience. It does not make them right or wrong; they are just from my experience and have helped me look at our world in a more compassionate supportive ideal to live my life by.

Science has proven the rest of the views and theories expressed in this book and should be accounted as general truths by the preponderance of the evidence presented. I believe some day when we move beyond our need to be right and consider everyone's need to be happy we will witness science prove this hypothesis of the power of human consciousness.

After all, humans on this planet share but a few common threads;

- We all feel the need to be loved
- We all feel the need to feel fulfilled
- and we all feel the need to be happy.

It is simplicity at its finest and yet has a complexity far beyond our current grasp unless we all begin to ask the question, "WHY".

Chapter One

THE FORMULA FOR A SUCCESSFUL LIFE

Sometimes, in our most desperate moments, there are desires that arise that will drive us forward to accomplish everything we ever wanted. The desire must always outweigh our fear which is keeping us from the very thing we want.

It is from this adversity that we gain great knowledge.

Napoleon Hill, author of 'Think And Grow Rich", stated, *"That from every Adversity, every heartache, every sorrow there is a seed of equal or greater benefit."*

This simple statement IS how we learn and grow or choose not to grow. If we can consciously overcome the subconscious fears we have been programmed with our whole life, then we stand a chance of changing situations before they become great adversities.

It wasn't until I read the book by Napoleon Hill called the "Law Of Success" that I began to understand the Scepters of Fear. I had been struggling with my own challenges around spirituality, money and relationships and miraculously the answers were revealed to me through the understanding of the basic fears that exist in most people.

The answer was in the subconscious programs that were running within us. Changing these programs can be the difficult part, positive affirmations do not work on a person that has been self-programmed to negatively react to a particular event.

Clearing the negative emotion programs that are running is paramount to having success. If you own negative emotions around money then you will struggle. If you own negative emotions around relationships then you will keep having the same difficulty. Remaining in negative emotions over long periods of time will most definitely affect your health. It is all about clearing the negative programs in your subconscious and then reprogramming the new life desired.

When I say "OWN" I mean that these programs, which you have picked up through learned behavior, are yours and can only be changed by you on an individual basis. It has been your interpretation of your environment that is giving you the results you are getting.

To disconnect 'you' from these learned programs it takes an understanding of the connections and then a systematic approach to clearing the counter-productive behavior and reprogramming the subconscious with a new behavior.

The Simplified Mathematical Success Formula

It has been discovered that there is but one simple formula for success, it is as follows;

$$YS = LoD + CH$$

YS is "Your Success" or your current result. What you have currently in your life is Your Success. I believe everyone is successful to their particular self-limitations, if they want more they need to change but 2 emotional things.

Part One of the formula; **LoD**, your "Level of Desire". How bad do you want it? Many of us have been taught not to dream, not to have any expectations from life because, "Life Is Hard!". "Being Successful is hard work" You have probably heard one of those sayings or something similar. When you are taught that life is a struggle, then of course most would give up before they ever started.

Perhaps, you have proved this to yourself already. You have tried and tried but just couldn't get to your goals. In turn you give up and settle back unhappily into your result. This is where life has beat you down and you think why ask for more because I am not worthy of having it. You can be completely oblivious to what the cause may be. If you are at that point in your life where you have given up trying then you have settled into your own self doubt and self loathing. It takes practiced skills to change your level of desire just as you have been practicing the self doubt thought patterns you have at this very moment.

The truth of the matter is that success is no more difficult than mediocrity; it is only a matter of choice.

Jim Rohn states, *"It is not the direction of the wind but the set of the sail that gets you to your destination." When we correct the errors of the past and set some new disciplines for the future, life changes.*

You get the good things you want in life when your Level Of Desire exceeds your fear and self doubt.

In other words . . .

When your Desire for what you want is strong enough, fear and false beliefs will take a back seat to your desire.

Part Two of the formula; **CH**, your "Current Habit". Current Habits are the programs that are constantly running in you that dictate your results. They are the anchors that tie you to you current result. These habits and believes have been reinforced with fear and doubt and the programs have become carved in stone.

To pictorially show you this formula I want to direct you to the following work of art on the next page by Nicholas Brooks (Yes, he is my very talented son).

This was Nicholas' perception of our struggle with self limitation and how we are held back by our emotional anchors, beliefs and past. He foresees we all have the capability of finding freedom when we break these chains. The things we desire are immediately in front of us and attainable.

A link to more of Nicholas' art can be found on our home page at www.GiveUpPain.com.

'The Angel Within' by Nicholas Brooks—2007

Most of our habits were built on fear or ill-gotten advice. In their over simplified form they would be like the following scenario;

LoD—A person really wants to be debt-free and living the good life. Modern teachings of the Law of Attraction states, *"Ask and it is given"*. Yet the result appears unchanging, "What could be wrong". The step that most people miss when they speak of Law of Attraction is the most important part; put yourself in a mental and emotional 'mode to receive' what you want. 'Ask' and then emotionally 'Allow' what you have asked for to come to you by 'Feeling' the joy of having what it is that you want.

So we are taught, through positive affirmations, to have happy thoughts and hopefully, with enough gloss on the day, we will get what we asked for. In the 'mode to receive' means; you need to put yourself in alignment with what you want as if you have already received it.

If your LoD has you wanting to be debt-free and living the good life . . . and your Current Habit (**CH**) has you spending money on lottery tickets instead of managing your money . . . It Usually Won't Happen because you are coming from the emotion of 'Lack of what you have'.

Let's add some clarity to the formula . . . Everyone is at their current level of Success. Your life is currently at the level of your desire and your current habits. In other words, if you don't dream of more and you sit on the couch watching TV brooding about how bad your life is, then your result is exactly matched to the equation.

Current Result; Poor Health
LoD; Wants better health, but not enough to change CH
CH; Eats all the wrong foods, does not exercise.

To get a new result, let's say great health, a person would need the desire to and emotional vision to see themselves as that fit person and then they will change their current eating and exercising habits.

How do you create desire in someone who has lost hope in themselves?

First remove the fear of moving out of their current habits. Make being uncomfortable, not such a bad thing. Get rid of the false perception and fear, where change equals 'Pain'.

Second create desire by learning how to dream and feel the wonderment of having what you want. Begin the belief in one's own abilities by understanding our own inner truths of how we feel about ourselves.

Not a bit of this can happen until YOU are first brutally honest with yourself. There is no escaping the formula it works every time. The sooner you can realize that you have the habits of your current success, the sooner you can begin to change them.

Someone who is broke needs to create the habit of feeling a prosperity consciousness, move towards simple Money Management skills and realize there is lots of abundance (money) for everyone.

Someone who wants to sell their product or service must overcome their fear of judgment from others, feel they are worthy and have the ability to develop their skills and personality. Knowledge is the path to empowerment.

Someone who wants health needs to see and feel themselves as a healthy person, study and practice good eating and exercising habits. So if you are sitting on the couch, feeling depressed around your body image, wishing your life was different and eating junk food, you really need to change your Current Habit.

Someone who wants world peace and does not see the beauty in our world will surely spend the rest of their days being unhappy until they find inner peace within themselves.

Your Success is equal to Your Level of Desire for what you want plus your movement towards new habits.

Overcome the Fear that holds you back and change your habits/programs.

Raise your Level of Desire by overcoming the Fears which have you believing you are not worthy of big dreams.

If you are in the state of mind of not being able to move forward then you are most likely in the state of 'Learned Helplessness' caused from years of habitual thinking and fear based beliefs which hold you back.

Learned helplessness is a psychological condition in which a human being or an animal has learned to believe that it is helpless in a particular situation. It has come to believe that it has no control over its situation and that whatever it does is futile. As a result, the human being or the animal will stay passive in the face of an unpleasant, harmful or damaging situation, even when it does actually have the power to change its circumstances. Learned helplessness theory is the view that depression results from a perceived lack of control over the events in one's life, which may result from prior exposure to (actually or apparently) uncontrollable negative events.

In the late 1950's a study was done where dogs were put in a maze and allowed to find their way through to the other side where there were doggy treats, fresh air, and grass; A real doggy heaven. Next the dogs were then strapped in at the starting gate and shocked with electricity if they tried to move forward. When the restraints were removed what surprised the scientists was the dogs would no longer go through the maze even though they knew how. Even shocking the dogs to get them to move did not work. This is how they coined the term "Learned Helplessness".

This same scenario is played out in the training of elephants. At a young age the baby elephants are chained to an anchored object where they are not allowed to move. They learn their freedom is the length of that chain. By the time the elephant reaches adulthood the chain is replaced by a small rope which the elephant could easily break. The elephant has learned that it is futile to struggle so it does not even try.

How bad has life been beating you up that your have learned nothing more than to stand in the starting gate limited by your emotional anchors with too much fear to move forward, knowing right in front of you there is great reward for little effort.

We have wasted too much of our lives focused on the negative within us all instead of the remarkable beings we can be.

**This is your life.
You are the Master of your Destiny,
the Captain of your Soul.**

—William Ernest Henley

Chapter Two

THE ROOT OF ALL FEAR

Fear of something is at the root of hate for others, and hate within will eventually destroy the hater.—George Washington Carver

I find this an interesting quote from Mr. Carver, our fear is the root for our own self hatred. What I have found to be true is *"What we hate in others, we hate within ourselves.".* We see in others the mirrored reflection of our own emotional turmoil. When we ask ourselves why we hate a particular person or why they upset us the most, we will find it is a reflection of what we hate or dislike about our own life. I should add, when we learn to become honest within ourselves. What we end up finding out is our hatred and dislike began as a seed planted from a fear or from our ignorance of compassion for others.

What we have discovered is the interconnection of all fears can be refined down to 2 basic Root fears or the 'Seed of All Fear' if you will. It is in the formation of these two Seed Fears we all have where all other fear develops a foothold. These 2 fears become the base ingredients in our recipe for a host of other root fears and phobias. Through our life events of emotions these ingredients can be mixed to produce any number of sub-fears and sub-phobias.

Think of yourself as the cake made from the base ingredients of flour & water. Neither flour nor water is much without the other. As we choose to build our mixture we may next add yeast and sugar.

Combinations of other spices or seasonings are added and then it is given time to bake to become what it will be.

Our volatile mixtures of emotions and fears given to us at a very early age in life, even inside the womb, will set our emotional compass for the rest of our lives until we learn how to identify them, understand them and rectify their effects on our mind, spirit and body.

It is important to understand . . . All emotions release chemical hormones in the body. These hormones become a type of fuel for the cells. These hormones can have a positive effect but some over long periods of time create an addictive response in the brain to produce more of the harmful chemicals. The physiological response we have to any particular emotion determines our health, wealth and happiness but, more on this later in the book.

As I stated, after much research, study, experimentation and consideration we have discovered the 2 basic ingredients of all Fear. They begin within us and determine our responses right from the time we are in the womb. After our birth the very substance of family life determines how you perceive your world and how you will react to any given circumstance. These early years develop the patterns we have for the rest of our lives unless we recognize them and consciously change the habits we have formed we will keep repeating them.

When I first discovered the concept of the Root Fears and began the journey in understanding my own inner fears it completely changed my perception of the world and my place in it.

Often times we only fear what we do not understand and comprehend. To conquer fear we must first take the journey in understanding it. Most fears are just false perceptions and really have no validity once you connect the dots on how you arrived at having the fear.

The Base Ingredients of FEAR!

Base ingredient one; The Fear of Darkness.

When we were performing our study of Fears on Emotions we found the word 'Darkness' does not do the emotional fear justice. Many people interpreted it as a fear of the Dark, which is not accurate.

The Fear of Darkness can also be interpreted as Emptiness. Some have stated it could also be interpreted as the Darkness within us or Evil.

Before we go further it is important to understand we all have the capability to perform good or bad deeds, it is the direction of our emotional compass that determines the result of our actions. Also it is only our perception of what is Good and what is Bad. There are not many truly evil or bad people out there, just people doing what they need to do to survive. Mankind receives far greater satisfaction preserving life and doing good deeds than it does being a destructive negative influence on other living creatures.

> **Doing Good Does You Good** – *Regular acts of altruism prolong our lives and improve our happiness. A study comprising of 2700 men over a long period of time, 10 years, found that men who engaged in regular volunteer activities had death rates half of those who did not. Altruistic effects include reduced stress; improved immune system functioning; a sense of joy, peace and well-being; and even relief from physical and emotional pain. These effects tend to last long after the helping encounter, and . . . with the frequency of altruistic behavior. Altruism is – unselfish regard for or devotion to the welfare of others*

Perhaps this fear began before we could understand our parent's language, before we could see or hear and before we could comprehend anything more than the darkness we were in within the womb. Some scientists and philosophers have determined this essence of fear to be from our very source, our soul prior to coming to this physical plain.

Whatever your beliefs are around this topic, one thing is undeniable. The emotions of the mother experienced by the child in the womb will either support this base fear or negate it.

A mother experiencing stress, self doubt or not feeling love for herself will release more Cortisol and Norepinephrine into her blood stream bombarding the fetus with these very same chemicals and produce the emotional feeling of emptiness within the unborn fetus.

Darkness or emptiness becomes the base ingredient for the child to experience the very same feelings of not being loved. As the child enters the world the perception and beliefs of the adult parents will now foster or quell this chemical reaction and addictive need of the child. The habitual chemical addiction has been set in place for root fears to blossom and grow within.

I do not for a moment believe that Mothers are to blame. There is no Blame to be had here. The process is set in place by our own ignorance of how our emotions affect us and every cell within our bodies. As a society we do not provide the means and the ability for a mother to receive the emotional, mental and physical support which is required to bring a young child into the world. We have taught mothers to be mindful of nutrition and toxins like cigarettes, drugs and alcohol however, we have never spoke of the need for emotional health through this process. It has just been within the last 20 years that discoveries were made showing the chemical effects of stress on the fetus.

New mothers need to be taught how to feel happiness, abundance and healthy choices throughout the pregnancy so these conditions are not set in place.

It is through our individual effort to be conscious and cognizant of our emotional state and feel the goodness of our nature at all times which is the way to resolve this condition within the mother, the fetus and most importantly within ourselves.

As with anything in our universe, there is a duality of nature. Hot vs. cold; up vs. down; Dark vs. Light. It has often been said we are but one of two states at any given time. "You are either growing or dying".

In this fear of Darkness a solution is found by using its opposite state of Light. Self Love is the Light we can shine within to overcome the Darkness and emptiness we may feel inside. To the habitual emotional response addict feeling self love can be the biggest challenge they can face. It is hard to love someone or some thing when you have spent so much time loathing them. Even if that person you loathed was yourself.

Darkness equals; emptiness, love-less-ness for self, dying, poor health, loneliness and feelings of an unfulfilled life. It is a disconnection from the truly amazing beings that we are.

Light equals; Self love, forgiveness of self, loving one's self despite what you may see in the mirror, good health, validated choices and growth. All these emotions are at the true root of who we are.

In the Darkness most living things do not grow. This base ingredient is how people are controlled by those who would 'keep you in the Dark', prevent you from learning new philosophies and seek knowledge to empower yourself.

All fear equals darkness, all love equals light. When we walk in a dark room we merely have to light a candle and the darkness flees away. You cannot bring a candle of darkness into an enlightened soul.

It is through our empowerment, our enlightenment that we can change those around us who are lost in the darkness of their physical life.

Base Ingredient two; The Fear of Pain

Of all the emotions that stop us from achieving and experiencing life to the fullest this has to be the most important base ingredient. Fear of Pain is a false perception of an anticipated result of our actions.

We will often use this fear as an excuse to not even try. I see this in large majority of adults today.

Outside of writing books I hold down different careers one of which is where I teach First Aid to people of all sizes, gender and from all walks of life. As part of the practical exercises students are asked to use a manikin we call "Choking Charlie". During this exercise they merely have to do abdominal thrusts on the manikin which forces a plastic ball out of the airway. It is not a difficult action and I have seen 8 year old children accomplish this without too much effort. The interesting point in this is when I see grown adults try and they cannot clear the obstruction. It is not that these people lack the physical capability of doing the exercise it is that their lack of confidence in themselves in front of other people which in turn holds them back, physically, and only validates the weakness they feel inside. It is fear of the pain of being ridiculed which overwhelms them. I usually explain this to the participants and validate them for the courage they have getting up in front of everyone and they can then do the exercise. It amazes me how we hold ourselves back from so many of life's simple pleasures and the joy of accomplishment when we allow these fears to run over our psyche and make us feel there is going to be a painful response.

Pain itself can be either physical or emotional. The physical pain of an injury is often forgotten within months. Child birth. For example, will once again see the parents procreate even though the physical pain was experienced during the first child's birth. Most times when we physically hurt ourselves we are reluctant to do the same thing over again which is a good thing and prevents us from damaging our bodies.

Fear of Physical pain is not a false perception but instead a survival mechanism which protects us. It is our Fear of Physical pain which prevents us from damaging the physical body and we often refer to that as 'Common Sense'. When you have had a physical injury caused from an action you did, it is common sense which prevents you from doing it again. If you placed you hand on a hot element by accident, the next time you were around that appliance you would be fully aware of what can happen if you do not pay attention.

However, Emotional Pain is different and is usually never forgotten. Ponder for a moment your emotional scars. They have the same physical effect on you today as they did when you were emotionally hurt. When you think of one of those past events in your life, you may still experience the tightness in your gut or a rush of humiliation that runs through you like goose bumps. These are the emotional scars you carry with you for a lifetime and just recalling them causes a noticeable uneasiness within your physical body.

In the mother who is stressed or experiencing feelings of emotional pain will once again produce a cocktail of hormones and chemicals in the body which in turn create these chemical addictions within the unborn fetus. Add to this the beliefs and perceptions of the parents after birth and the Fear of Pain is either supported in the child or, once again, negated.

Later in life how we react to our emotional pain, can cause a knee-jerk reaction where we feel the need to hurt others either physically or emotionally.

It is not our individual thoughts that are an enemy; it is our persistent wallowing in a particular thought-feeling that creates these base ingredients.

Even if the mother were in a supportive state of mind and emotion, emotional events after birth in the early development years (0 to age 6) can have lasting effects on the child. These early years are the most important times for development and future growth. The young child is a sponge devouring as much knowledge and perceptions as it can from its care givers. The child is learning how to survive in its environment by copying what it has learned. When I say copying I do not mean the literal sense of mimicking what they are taught but instead they will create situations where the emotional outcome will give them that same chemical feeling.

It is only through our understanding of our emotional pain and the realization that our words hurt others who have their own emotional pain where we will finally become more compassionate human beings, supportive of ALL living things on this planet.

I do not believe that people are maliciously hurting us, emotionally, because they are evil, it is just what our human nature may have become and the habits we may have learned when we are full of our own emotional pain inside.

I do not expect, as a society, we will be able to change these beliefs in a short period of time. However, over generations we can set in motion a more supportive positive emotional experience for new parents that will change our children's perception of the world we live in.

The great news is you will be taught in this book how to overcome the base and root fears laid down prior to you ever having memory of how you got them in the first place.

Building a Recipe Of Root Fears

The base ingredients are now in place and with support of the parents and the influence of our physical surroundings the roots are now free to grow off in many directions. The root fears we have identified and worked with show they can be a direct combination of either or both of the base ingredient fears. As you read the following fears consider how you have been affected through out your life by those around you.

The words and actions of your parents and peers have formed the perceptions you hold within you at this current time. Through understanding the root fears and how they are formed backed by the life experience you have led to this point make up 'who' you are and the current life results you are experiencing.

As with any Fear the longer we hold on to it the more rooted and divided it becomes. Not unlike a weed, a fear will branch off and pop up in different areas of our life giving us results we feel are fate in many cases. We often hear people say I am destined to be this way or that way which is not true it is merely the fact the root of the challenge you are experiencing has never been resolved by you.

It has taken root within you from a seed of these two very basic fears.

We will begin by identifying each root fear and then build on the sub-categories from there. It is interesting to study this list to decipher for yourself the root of where your particular fear or phobia came from.

Base Ingredient	Root Fear	Sub-Root Fear	Learned Helplessness
DARKNESS	Fear of Death	Fear of Falling	Fear of animals Dogs, Snakes, etc.
	Fear of Being Alone	Fear of Old age	
	Fear of Losing Love		Fear of Insects
PAIN	Fear of Judgement	Fear of Public Speaking	Fear of Failure
	Fear of Authority	Fear of Doctors/ Dentists/Police	Paranoia/most phobias
	Fear of Poverty	Fear of Change	Fear of Moving Forward

As we study and look at these few root fears you will begin to see they are based on our perception of the world and our belief system that we were raised with. Most of the belief perceptions you were given, other than physical harm warnings from your parents, were perceptions based on their beliefs and not their experience.

Things, in the broad general statement, if not personally experienced are nothing more than myths and perceptions given to you by another person.

These root fears are how you are organized, ruled and sold to by parents, religion, government, corporations and all advertising.

The Fear of Death

Our first fear to cover is the fear of Death. It is an interesting fear because we know 'Death' applies to every living animal and plant based thing on the planet. It is inescapable and so we have tried to find some comfort in our interpretation of what happens when we die. We have spent so much time fearing our perception of this dark empty void that we often become incapacitated to do anything with our lives. The fear itself derives from our lack of knowledge of what happens to us after death.

Religion teaches us that after death there is an afterlife and if you live according to the dogma of the church you will be saved and live eternally in heaven. If you are bad your soul will either cease to exist or you will spend eternity atoning for your sinful life.

Atheism teaches when you are dead . . . You Are Dead! The life force from your body ceases to exist and your body becomes fuel for anything that will consume it.

Most other modern philosophies feel that when you die your energy lives on in some other state and returns to physical world through reincarnation of some sort. Energy, according to Albert Einstein, cannot be destroyed, so if the essence of who we are, our soul, is of pure energy then it must live on in some conscious state after we have left this physical body. The interesting thing about the body's energy system (spirit) is, it cannot currently be measured with scientific tools that are recognized by conventional science and yet we all knowingly feel we have a spiritual consciousness which is inside us right now.

The plain and simple truth is, no one truly knows what lies on the other side of death but one thing is for sure, the general consensus is that there is some sort of life after physical death. That would mean there is no real death just the death of the physical body and not the energy or soul essence of who you are.

In my travels I have spoken to many 'mediums' which are in contact with the non-physical world. Undeniably they have all shared with me, there is no hell when we leave this physical plain only a heaven of true forgiveness, love and compassion. These same 'mediums' have shared, the biggest regret after passing from the physical world those souls felt was they should have been more forgiving, loving and compassionate while they were alive on this plain. This is often the message delivered to family members who are searching for contact with their passed loved ones.

Time spent being angry, depressed or bitter is wasted time that could have been better spent enjoying every moment of every day and enjoying every person they came in contact with appreciating them for the loving compassionate souls we all have living within us.

In my experience, I have felt the presence of my father since he passed when I was still a boy and more recently when my mother passed away I could feel her presence around me and even smell her unique 'Avon' perfume every now and then. I know they are there with me because of the comfort they provide to me when life throws me a challenge.

My brother asked me one time, many years after my father's death, "You must have hated him (Dad) for leaving you at such an early age?" I replied, "Not at all! We never argued or fought, I always tried to live to a standard where I felt my father would have been proud of me, AND, I always felt he was with me helping me through my challenges and enjoying my accomplishments."

I felt my father, even though he was not physically here, was proud of the person I have become and the people I have helped along my life journey.

I do not believe in evil spirits that is the stuff that makes for Hollywood movies and religious fear mongering, after all, if you are not afraid of what will happen to you in the afterlife how can you be controlled in this physical life by those who would benefit from your fear.

Whatever your perception of what death is we all know it is inevitable.

What you should allow to drive you is, to live a fulfilled life here and now. Whether you are eternal conscious souls or only have these few moments in this physical world, making the most of it and enjoying the journey should be your intention.

I feel confident in saying, you know this feels like a supportive perspective deep inside you. Your inner voice says there is 'something' far beyond anything we can perceive here in this physical life.

To quote Abraham-Hicks, *"There is no Life & Death only Life & Life!"*

Learn to Live your Life to the fullest and do not regret the decisions you have made in the past. If you are living a life of regrets now, then now, is the time to change that.

If you could see, as I do, the greatness you have inside of you, you would know that we are eternal beings who have the ability to change our perception and our philosophy to one that supports the ideal of living a full and happy life. After all, isn't that what we all want . . . To be Happy!

The Fear of Being Alone

In the darkness there are only our naked thoughts and feelings of who we 'Think' we are. The fear of being alone comes from our lack of confidence in ourselves and not being aware of the true power we all have within us. 'Being alone' would mean perhaps; you were socially unacceptable and not worthy of other people. Your thoughts and perceptions were not accurate. When you feel good you know you can feel the presence of so much more energy within you.

We are designed to be social creatures and not lone wolfs. It is in the power of friendships and other relationships where we find the co-creative process. However, today, we are taught to be individual competitive consumers, which is out of harmony with 'Life' as a whole.

In recent scientific studies it was shown that people in North America report they feel alone more so now then 30 years ago. Our culture teaches that we are all "Special" and we must compete to rise above the masses. The by product of this thinking is loneliness for the achievers and isolation for the non-achievers. The truth is 'you' are no more 'special' than any other human on this planet. You may be unique in your perspective, perceptions and experiences, you may be gifted enough to realize the capabilities we all have within us and you may even be able to use your gifts and talents better than the next person, but that does not mean that they (the next person) cannot do the very same thing if they were to change their perceptions of themselves.

A single cell by itself is nothing much really, but a community of cells in the body can make up an organ like the heart or lungs. Those communities of organs make up the person that we are. The people that we are make up the communities that we live in and the different cultures we build. Those cultures make up the countries and life force of our planet. Our planet is amongst a community of other planets which make up our solar system which is part of our galaxy and so on. Life is ever expanding from a single cell in your body to the cosmos of the universe.

Since the beginning of mankind we were a tribal people's working together in harmony and with a sense of community. We were not meant to survive this life journey without the interaction with others. It is cooperative creative growth we all desire.

To overcome this fear adopting a philosophy of becoming active within your community and meeting new people is paramount. As we, humankind, survive so does our legacy and our altruistic intention.

As we connect with others we get to feel the co-creative process at its best in sharing ideas and philosophies, emotions and physical contact. Remember the last time you visited with a friend and how in reminiscing you both felt so good. Or the last time you and a co-worker got together to resolve a challenge facing your company.

Understand there is a need for you to be social it is the basis of all life on the planet.

When I reflect on the elderly people I have met that yearn for death to take them away, it is usually because they have lost their sense of purpose and the co-creative process which was lost from having a small circle of friends and influences.

Years ago when I was a paramedic we could almost wager that when one person died their spouse would soon turn sick and it would not be too long after they too would die. I can remember the look in the eyes of the senior citizens I picked up in the ambulance who were left alone. You could feel they were lonely and felt passed over by life. It was very sad to experience that emptiness they were enduring at the time. Often times we and the rest of the emergency medical services teams were this person's only social contact. They were often forgotten by their family, with few surviving friends left, and inhibited by their illness to get out and meet other people. It is this knowing of life in its later stages where I feel we develop a good part of this fear of being alone.

A nurse friend of mine who worked with the elderly asked me one time to promise if she ever got that old and lonely to kill her. She said she never wanted to be placed in a 'Old Folks Home' where she would be forgotten and then slowly wither and die.

Perhaps that is what the coming of death is to all of us. Perhaps it is a feeling of being alone and being forgotten and then we finally choose to leave the physical plain and go back home to where we know we are loved.

*   *   *

In my experience I have found, in quiet moments by myself, there is great reflection and connection going on with the non-physical world. It is my time to quiet the confusion in the conscious mind and slip into the peacefulness of a subconscious meditative state where clarity and creativity begins to develop. That development happens because of the co-creative process caused by the many different points of view and experiences others have shared with me. If I had restricted myself from meeting new people and making new friends my thoughts and perceptions of this world would have been stunted in their growth.

There is a great need for us all to expand and grow through developing relationships with others. The 'Fear' that holds us back from meeting new people is the fear of rejection or the fear of not being loved. There is a wonderful community building in our world right now, it is the community of social networking. When we connect through these networking sites we can discover that there are millions of people around the world that share our feelings and experiences. It is a place where we can gain our voice and help change the world. It can also be a place where we can carry our bitterness and limited beliefs to have a negative effect. When we use any form of communication and connection with others it must be to help empower ourselves through knowledge and understanding and help those around us to become more compassionate to the wrong that may be happening in our world.

These are great times we live in where we no longer have to feel alone in our thoughts and feelings when there is so much power in the co-creative process found with others.

Seek out knowledge, Learn, Grow and help change the world we live in by changing your perspective of the way the universe works.

The Fear of Losing Love

This fear was one of my challenges. I used to do things so that other people would like me. It was a very misguided way to live my life for this point is true, you cannot make everyone happy. I also discovered I became bitter after a few failed relationships and friendships. You see it was easier for me to shut off all emotions so that I would not have that feeling of not being loved. The challenge with thinking that way is you also shut yourself off to all the joy love can bring you when you do allow it into your heart.

We have been taught that we are nothing without another's love and we do very bizarre things to get attention which we have been misguided to believe is getting love. The fear of losing love can also be equated to the fear of being rejected by another.

Culturally we have been taught, for the most part, to be complete we need to find a life partner to make us whole. Marriage is the obvious result of that perception but not necessarily the correct perception. I do not want you to think I have anything against marriage.

My wife and I have been together for over 32 years, the amazing thing about our relationship is that we are wholly and soulfully independent people who really love and enjoy each others company. However, I do understand that not all relationships can be like that and it should not be a goal to find Mr. or Miss Right until you have learned how to feel complete within yourself. It is a misguided dogma to believe that we are not whole unless we have some other person to love. It is a false perception delivered to us from our early youth.

Parents used the fear of losing love to get you to behave to their standards;
"Be good or Santa will not bring you presents.",
"If you keep acting bad Mommy and Daddy will be very upset with you".

We have been programmed to think that Love can be taken away from us at any time if we do not give up our power to someone else.

It becomes a "Learned Helplessness" we develop around this fear which will keep a person in a relationship even though they are suffering some type of physical or emotional abuse.

Love itself has become so contaminated with all the different perceptions around it that most people, when asked, cannot even describe what Love is. In one of our workshops we would ask people a few questions around this topic of 'Love'.

First, describe how they knew if someone loved them, and most answers came back as, "feeling appreciated".

Secondly, How could your partner or friend show you that they love you or appreciate you? This question often drew blank stares or they would revert back to the same answer as question 1, very confusing for some. The lines became very convoluted.

It appears as psychologists have been saying for years there a few different personality groups where people react differently in different situations.

For example; One couple I had the opportunity to work with had ended their marriage after a couple of decades. The chronic reason for this was that each one did not feel appreciated in the relationship. When I asked the one partner, *"Did your husband ever tell you that he loved you?"* she replied, *"Yes, but I don't believe what people say they are usually lying to get something."*

I continued with the question, *"How would he show you that he loved you then?"* her reply was, *"If he loved me he could have given me a hug or a kiss on the cheek every now and then."*

When the husband was asked if he loved his ex-wife he explained that he loved her very much but she would never return his love. *"I used to tell her all the time that I loved her and she would never respond or she would give me this funny look."* He said. I asked him if he ever thought of giving her a hug or kiss when he came home from work. His reply was, *"I am not into all that mushy stuff."*

Here were two people who loved each other and did not know how to communicate their love with each other.

Some people feel loved when they hear (Auditory) the words. Others feel loved by the physical connection (Kinesthetic) of touch like a hug or kiss. And yet others feel loved when their partner can show their love (Visual) by buying them flowers or cleaning up the house.

Take a moment to ponder these questions. Do you know how to communicate your love to that certain person in your life?

Are they auditory, kinesthetic or visual people?

How does someone show or prove to 'You' that they love you?

In turn, because we do not understand these relationship communication variables we often fear losing what we currently have. When all we really have to do is learn how to communicate with our partner and the fear is then gone.

This brings me to the final understanding of the topic of Fear of Losing Love . . .

Because of human nature we get far more satisfaction in being good than we do at being bad. We feel more satisfied giving to someone than we do from receiving something from another. Perhaps we should be pondering the conclusion that we are Givers of Love and not Getters of love. When we crave the false attention to 'Get' love we often end up in relationships that do not work. When we learn the language of Love and how to give it to others we feel more love inside not only for the people we have relationships with but on a deeper level, more love for ourselves.

We see this play out in children who have been conditioned to think that 'getting attention' equals 'getting love' especially when there is another sibling involved. The child will act out to get the parents attention and all the while they are doing this 'bad' behavior they are actually pushing the parents love away.

When I work with children who are having behavioral challenges the very first question I ask them is 'Why' are they acting out, are they angry or frustrated with someone? On one occasion we had a young lady come to us for counseling. She had done some destructive things around the house because her parents had locked her out of the house and in retaliation the parents used 'Tough Love' to have the young woman charged by the police for the destruction of their property and it created a lot of animosity between the parents and the child. The young woman seemed to feel she had deserved it. I commented that I do not believe in 'Tough Love', she became distressed and snapped at me asking how I would have dealt with that situation. I told her the first question I would ask you, if you were my child is, *"Sweetheart, why are so angry?"* The young woman's eyes welled up with tears and she said, *"Nobody has ever asked me that before."* You see, to me, we do not need to use 'Tough Love' to teach our children a lesson, it is usually because they are not feeling loved in the first place which causes them to act out. Developing our communication skills with children at an early age keeps the lines of communication open so when children are expressing themselves using the need for attention we can talk to them openly and honestly about what it will take to resolve the hurt emotions. Often times what parents will find out is that the child may be experiencing emotional turmoil at school or from their peers or siblings and are merely venting their anger or frustration the only way they know that will bring them relief.

You often heard it said, *"We only hurt the ones we love."* Ask yourself if that phrase is supportive and loving and you will discover this is another false perception we use to cover up the fact we do not know how to communicate our feelings and our fear.

If you knew the person you were talking to was a kinesthetic type personality and you made an effort to touch them or hug them, you would make their heart melt with the feelings of love towards you. You would feel far more rewarded and loved yourself in the giving.

The same rule applies to our self. Learning to love yourself can be challenging to the majority of people today. Doing loving things for 'You' is very important to overcoming these deep roots of this fear.

If you are an 'Auditory' type personality, tell yourself out loud, *"I Love Myself"*

A Kinesthetic type personality, Get a massage or learn how to massage or lovingly touch your own body.

For the Visual type personality, do something that would show you loved yourself.

The fear of Losing Love or not being loved is really a bunch of false perceptions we, as a society, have developed around "What love is".

I am not sure of 'Why' it is, however, the fear of losing love appears to be tied directly to the Fear of Insects like spiders and other bugs. When we taught people how to reduce the Fear of Losing Love or not being loved, the Fear of Insects also went away. On more than one occasion when a client would say they had a fear of a particular insect and were asked what it was about that insect they disliked so much, the answers came back as a feeling of disgust in some manner. When we asked if the person was disgusted with themselves, the answer was, yes. It was not so much a fear of Losing Love but a feeling of the Love they had lost for themselves due to some emotional event in their early years.

Learning to 'Love' and 'Forgive' yourself is key to dispelling this false perception and many other fears. You will have to trust me when I say, *"You are worth loving. You are unique and you are needed as part of the harmony of this earth."* I have seen the power in so many people to become what truly lies within their heart. I know we are all Good people and worth so much more than we give ourselves credit for.

Understand these key elements around Love; All human beings worldwide share these things in common,

1. the need to be loved and
2. the energy which runs through us all which some people call God Source.

These elements are the root of building our world society to one that works in harmony with us all. It is not the need for money, government, religion, power, or to be right. It is our common desire to be loved. It must begin with you for if you cannot love yourself, what sort of chance does humanity stand.

I have found that the key to learning to love yourself is in allowing yourself to be loved. Later in this book you will be taught how to use a technique called EFT. In the 'Setup' part of using EFT we use words like, "I Love and Accept Myself". Those words become very powerful in our healing. Many times I have worked with clients where just saying those words would bring them to tears. As we cleared the negative emotions of loving ones self and they began to allow themselves to be loved, miracles would happen in their bodies.

You could see the change in their expression and the sparkle in their eyes would return as if they were being reborn. Of course the pain they may have been experiencing would go away and not return.

Learning to love yourself FIRST is paramount to never having to give up your power to some other person ever again.

We all came from love, we will all return to love, our journey is to enjoy the loving feeling we can hold for ourselves within us. It is so powerful!

The Fear of Judgment (Criticism)

This is one of our deepest and most popular fears amongst the masses. This is the key root fear with people who have a fear of public speaking. We are taught how to judge others at a very early age. We judge people on how they look, dress, talk and walk. We judge them on every physical attribute they have. It is our way of understanding ourselves and our place in the physical world. We end up associating with those who are most like us and like bands of lions, we pounce on every difference that others may have to ours.

Religious groups are taught to judge other religions as having it all wrong even though they both worship the same God. We find the differences and we are taught to hate that in others instead of using those differences to find a newer harmony within ourselves. We maliciously criticize each others beliefs when there has been no absolution for one belief to claim dominance over the other. Wars have been created over our religious beliefs even though the number one charter of all religious commandments is *"Thou shall not kill"*.

We only hate in others what we most fear in ourselves because if we were wrong on one thing could it be we are wrong on many other things too. We have been taught by our society to look for the differences the oddballs, so to speak, and to chastise them for being different in their looks and their philosophies. It was formed thousands of years ago when our communities were our tribes. It was a way of protecting our tribe from the influences of other tribes.

This Fear holds us back from accomplishing success with the bitter questioning of our own self esteem. *"If I do this what will others think of me?"*

The interesting point of this fear is . . . We All Judge each other! Usually the ones who most fear being judged or criticized are the very ones who judge and criticize others the most. This reminds of Shakespeare's play Hamlet where there is a line which reads;

"The lady doth protest too much, methinks." The phrase has come to mean that one can "insist so passionately about something not being true that people suspect the opposite of what one is saying."

I find myself thinking this when I hear people call other people liars or accuse them of being a thief or are critically judging another. What usually happens, in time, we find the accusers were the very same people who were doing most of the lying and stealing. When it came to judging others they were also the very same people who were insecure about themselves.

There is emotional relief in knowing it does not matter what we do or how we look because we will be judged whether we do or whether don't.

"Damned if I do and Damned if I don't"

I was taught by my parents to only judge others on how we ourselves would like to be judged. This phrase, in essence, came from the bible and as part of the churches moral doctrine and it would suggest that the job of 'Judgment' should be left to only God. And yet, here we stand as mortal humans judging each other on who is right and who is wrong, who will rise to heaven and who will be cast into hell for their actions. The mere action of judging suggests those offenders should be measured by their own rule and when I explain this to them they find themselves less critical of others because of their own inner fear of being judged by God.

This is the morally saddest of all fears, overcoming this fear would help us celebrate and appreciate the differences we all have and be compassionate enough to at least try and understand another's point-of-view or cultural differences before casting our judgment on them. In attempting to understand and communicate with others we open ourselves up to a world of knowledge and we could leave hatred behind.

The moral high ground on this point would be understand nobody can say they have all the right answers. Even from the point of view of this book, I can only suggest techniques and understanding which may help you find the answers within yourself and evolve emotionally as the true wonderful spirit that you are.

The beauty we hold in our hearts is far greater than the beauty portrayed through our physical appearance and yet our own judgment of ourselves does not allow us to see our inner beauty, we become superficial and shallow in our personality. I have had the opportunity to work with many physically beautiful human beings and yet on the inside they despised their own reflection in the mirror. On the other hand I have worked with people less physically attractive and their personality shines like a beacon which draws everyone to their light.

We all have the capability to be beautiful beyond the limitations of our physical appearance. As we leave behind the cruel judgment we hold for ourselves and others we discover the beauty within and the beauty within others. As we lose our fear of what others may think of us we discover the infinite way we can view ourselves and our surroundings finding only beauty in all things and all situations.

Cast no Stones at others for they may be the reflection of ourselves we need to heal.

The Fear of Authority

The fear of authority is challenging to explain without actually creating more fear within you. However, it is through your understanding of this fear and your journey in discovering some new truths which will help you overcome the fear itself.

This is the very fear others will instill in us to control us. It is an unguided conspiracy against humanity to benefit a few. I do not want to sound too cynical here, but there are things you become aware of as you study and analyze the roots of fear. If I asked you if you had a fear of authority you would probably not even recognize and yet it runs deep within our culture. This fear which is a culmination of many fears put together and uses the seed of 'Pain' as its source.

We are taught from a very young age to respect authority figures, for example; police, teachers, preachers, doctors, celebrities, corporations and government. We are taught those organizations and people have our best interests and humankind's best interests at heart and we dare not challenge them for fear of being reprimanded. We are taught that without them there would be anarchy and society would fall apart. All of these points are not necessarily true though.

This can be a valid fear within people because truly the outcome would be painful if we went against the rules. We spend our days looking over our shoulder waiting for the boogey man to come and get us. Near paranoia appears to be the normal these days and it is in this confusion where the very thing we fear gains more power and a deeper hold on our psychological state.

To maintain this control over the masses we are bombarded with propaganda through the media, in our schools and churches. They have even taught us to report anyone who goes against their law and authority because they, the authority, are there to protect and educate us all.

We have become so complacent in this dogma of trust we actually believe these groups are looking out for us. We have reached a point culturally where we turn to our governments, churches and law makers to run our lives for us.

It is our fear of authority that runs so deep within us that we do not dare question and make ourselves aware of another way of thinking that change us all culturally for the better.

Imagine you have been brought up in a culture with beliefs that are not to be questioned. The authority states, *"To question their laws is an act of treason punishable by death or even worse punishment to your very soul after death"*.

The fear mongering that is handed down has a soul purpose of controlling 'You' so that you do not question their decisions. Think of it as enslavement of the populous by enslaving their minds. The fear mongering works so well we, in an attempt to control the aspects of our life, adopt the very same fear based tactics in an attempt to control those within our very reach, our loved ones.

Parents use the Fear to make sure you behave, not because you are necessarily doing something wrong but instead because you are not doing things to make 'them', the parent(s) happy.

I witnessed this being played out by a young mother. Her daughter asked if she could go outside and play, the mother said "NO!", not because there was any problem with going outside other than it would have meant that the mother would have to get up, turn off the TV and go out with her. Instead the mother chose to tell the little girl that she was afraid someone would abduct her and molest her even though this could not be further from the truth. This was in a rural community, on a large lot where no one could enter without being noticed. The false perception of being hurt or killed was used by the mother to get what she wanted and not what was good for the child. This is how we have learned to use 'Authority' to instill fear in others to get them to do what we want or what makes us happy and is not co-creative in satisfying both parties needs.

When our authority is questioned we either retaliate through violent actions or withdraw and stubbornly defend our decision with dogma that has no scientific basis or factual evidence. We, in essence, are cornered like a dog and feel the need to defend our position however false it may be.

Understanding this, you can see that the fear of authority is merely a learned habit which has been passed down through culture, government and religion.

Awakening from this false fear is first recognizing what the authority figure is attempting to control and why they are using fear mongering. It is manipulation, to get you to do what others want you to do and not necessarily what you want to do. We all want to be happy and feel loved so why do we feel the need to use others to make us happy.

The truth of the matter is no one person or group has the authority or dominion to rule over another human being. The truth is with this type of fear mongering there is always a dollar or measure of value involved. Follow the value and you will find that some corporation, bank or individual is benefiting from your fear in some way.

In a recent article written by Foster Gamble founder of the Thrive Movement he noted that when things don't feel right in our culture there is generally something to be gained by some by oppressing the majority. His case was when you follow the money you will find a basic formula that is used to make the masses compliant and accepting of your agenda without even noticing what they are losing. This began with religions hundreds of years ago where people were controlled through fear to be compliant with the rules of the church. Government was next in line to adopt these principals in populous control. Today we see corporations use this on a large scale to control government and the people. Finally, we as individuals have learned how to use this fear formula to get what we want from others, the only challenge with that is most people do not follow the formula with the planning and accuracy which is required and they end up getting too caught up in the negative aspects of the game.

The formula for controlling others, be that individuals, consumers or cultures is always the same, to create a "Problem-Reaction-Solution".

Step one, according to Mr. Gamble, create or capitalize on a problem.

- In government we point our fingers at another country that has what we want (oil or other resources).
- Corporations use this by identifying a new illness or mental disorder which they can categorize.

Step Two, Incite a fearful reaction.

- Governments will use propaganda to instill fear in their people by telling them these other countries are out to get them and they will surely kill us if we do not preemptively strike first.
- Corporations will also use this same tactic to monger fear about pandemic outbreaks of disease or point out something obscure and then demonize it.

Step Three; Implement an already prepared plan and previously unacceptable 'solution' that further centralizes control.

- Governments will send the poor off to fight these false wars while they, the elite, become wealthy. Or, they will use this as an opportunity to take away our rights as individuals.
- Corporations will use this for planned obsolescence of their products so that new ones need to be purchased.

It is much like in days gone by when a conman would create a distraction while his team of accomplices would go through the crowd and pick the pockets of distracted people. This recipe of using fear while picking the pockets of the unaware is common place in our society today.

The malicious use of this fear on the masses goes against the grain of our very existence. These mongers of fear create more stress, death, and negative emotions than any other thing on earth.

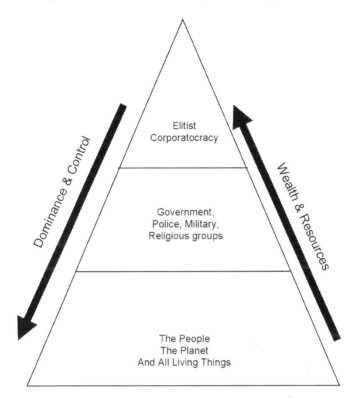

There would be no anarchy if governments collapsed. Governments were formed out of anarchy to protect the people. Today governments protect corporations and banks and use fear and dominance to enforce their will on us. Governments have become Imperialistic forces ruling over the people who first conceived and put them in to place to protect the masses not suppress them.

In our educational system we do not teach people how to think but instead teach them what to think. If any individual grows at a faster rate than others or displays any characteristic outside the 'normal' rules they are deemed 'abnormal' and forced down to comply with the guidelines of the educational institution. The term "Cutting the Tall Poppy" or 'Tall Poppy Syndrome' describes a social phenomenon in which people of genuine merit are resented, attacked, cut down, or criticized because their talents or achievements elevate them above or distinguish them from their peers. In the classroom, people who excel beyond the group, are impulsive, overactive or people who learn through different methodologies are frowned upon and considered unruly or that there is a learning disorder involved like Attention Deficit Hyperactivity Disorder (ADHD). In this case the student is judged as having a mental disability, given medications to curb their behavior without ever testing to see if perhaps they may just have a different way of learning.

I encourage you to watch the documentary entitled 'The Marketing Of Madness' produced by Citizens Commission on Human Rights for a more in-depth look at how psychotropic drugs are used to control the masses.

Most people learn in different manners, some can read books, others learn from seeing pictures explaining the theory while others need to be able to put their hands on something to comprehend how it works. Other learning methods are not even considered when it comes to teaching the general populous. In our work with people suffering dyslexia we found there was always a way to teach the person dependant on their particular learning behavior.

We often have opportunity to work with young adults to help them deal with fear, stress and emotional issues.

One of my personal favorite stories to share is in regards to two young ladies who were told they had forms of Attention Deficit Hyperactivity Disorder or ADHD. They were being prescribed medication to control their class disruptions and angry outbursts towards the teaching staff. The interesting discovery was that the girls both had the ability to read 650 to 850 words per minute which is nearly 4 times the normal rate of an adult at 200 words per minute. The average adult (teacher) speaks at 120 words per minute. These young people were consuming information faster than any teacher could deliver the topic, it was no small surprise that they were not abnormal as the doctors & teachers would have us believe. They were not even the "normal", they were above normal and were simply bored. When we taught them how to control their emotional outbreaks of frustration their grades greatly improved and there was no need for any medications to dull their thinking. The new normal for our youth is their wonderful ability to consume information at speeds far beyond what we, society, have the ability to teach them. Our youth are not defective our education system is defective. And yet, here we are still trying to control them through outdated methodologies and drugging.

We should remind our oppressors that we are human beings not 'sheeple' that need to be controlled. This is the one great fear that is holding our civilization back from advancing and growing as it should.

We need to remind ourselves of the liberated times when;

- ➢ Governments spoke on our behalf, the people, not corporatocracy and lobby groups;
- ➢ Police were there to 'Serve and Protect' all people not the wealthy corporations who design laws and systems which do not provide the essentials of life for all people.
- ➢ Teachers taught children to be creative and how to manage money instead of going deep into debt to afford a limited education and become nothing more than consumers or the mechanical gears of a corporate run society;
- ➢ Religions promoted peace, compassion and love not 'end times' and that an enemy of their doctrine should be killed in holy wars. "Thou Shall Not Kill";
- ➢ Doctors swore an oath to never poison their patients with chemicals that upset the natural balance of the body and they promoted natural healing methodologies that were in alignment with our bodies and humanity's needs not 'Big Pharma's' needs.

The way to overcome this fear is to know your rights, seek knowledge. If something does not feel right then it probably isn't.

Understand any person or group acting under the guise of authority do not have your best interests at heart only theirs. Your duty is to yourself and your understanding that in many ways we are all selfish and want what is best for ourselves and sometimes we do this by trying to force others to be responsible for our happiness.

That, however, is contradictory to the way the universe works and we need to aware of this fact so we can better appreciate all people and living things.

The Fear of Poverty

"We don't understand what we really need so we fall prey to manic substitution desires"—Epicurus

This Fear could almost be described as a fear of isolation because nothing makes a person feel more inadequate than not being able to make enough money to take care of themselves and their family. We create so much stress in our lives around money it only seems to take us further away from the very thing we want more of. There is also a feeling of being alone in this and that nobody else is having financial challenges. We have been taught that money DOES buy happiness if only we consume more and buy more stuff.

However, there is a false premise around money and the belief 'more will make us happier'. In actuality more money does not make you 'more happy' especially if getting it goes against an ethical foundation the vast majority of people have within their very soul.

We have a fear of being judged by what we have, not, who we are. This fear creates anger and hatred within ourselves and against others. So much so that we will do nearly anything to get what we think we need.

In most people, including the wealthy people, this can create a guarded reaction and near paranoia that someone is out to get your stuff.

It is the basis of building Darwinian capitalism so that the strong can survive. But, nothing shows us more that we are out of harmony with something than our fear of poverty or not having enough money. Once again this is a learned perspective that is not true.

We are taught to look down on the 'have-not's and to idolize the very rich. Yet at the same time we have this inner battle going on because we have also been taught that money is the root of all evil or rich people are bad.

This one fear causes us to do things that are interpretively unethical to attain more of what we do not have and become closed off to others who are experiencing the very same fear. We attempt to justify our actions as being moral when deep inside we can feel the great imbalance this causes within.

There is no difference between the person who would steal to feed their family or the person who would sell you lies to feed their family. I have over the course of many years listened as people redefine the saying of "Money is the root of all evil" to clarify that it is the "Love of money that is the root of all evil" and then try and sell you some worthless product or knowledge so they can make a dollar. Money or the Love of money is NOT the root of all evil, People and our fear is. Money can be used to do a lot of bad things however it can better be used for doing good things if we allowed ourselves to see that.

Bill Hicks Comedian quoted, "I do not believe making money in order to consume goods is mankind's sole purpose on this planet. I believe our purpose on this planet has to do with creating and sharing"

Money is a tool and can be compared to a knife. We can use a knife to slice vegetables, carve beautiful works of art or protect ourselves from an animal attack. We can also use a knife as a weapon to steal or meme another person. It is the type of person we are and our use of the tool that determines our morality.

We have come to believe we live in a constant belief state of lack and limitation. When the truth of the matter is exactly the opposite, we live in a world of abundance and well-being if only we would allow ourselves to see this we would not feel the need to compete for limited dollars.

The challenge with poverty is, we live in a monetary society where everything depends on 'You' making money. The biggest reason you may not have as much as you want is because you were not taught how money truly works and how our emotional state around the topic has a causal effect on how much we get.

These past few years we have heard lots of talk around the 'Law of Attraction' and how you can use it to get more money. So you buy the courses, go to the workshops, meditate daily, get into 'get rich quick' schemes and still nothing changes. Once again you feel there is something wrong with you and you feel you are alone in your battle with poverty.

The truth is there is a biological chemical reason for this happening within your body that keeps you having more money. You create it from the stress and fear you have around trying to attain more with unsuccessful results. Fear creates stress, stress causes the body to produce chemical hormones that your body becomes addicted to and you produce the same results. The fear of poverty you have is not there because there is something wrong with you or you are lazy it is because you have created patterned thinking habits which keep producing the same results over and over again.

To clear the behavioral patterns it is best to understand the truth around 'How' our money system works and reinforce the belief that money is just another tool. It is 'we' who determine how to use the tool.

At our very core we are compassionate beings with a heart and soul that resonates when we give to others and love others. And yet here we are dependant on a system that teaches competitiveness and a disconnection between the masses.

According to Dr. David Suzuki *"We have been taught the 'Economy' is the most important thing, yet, it (the Economy) is not alive. It does not laugh, it does not feel, it does not consider humanity and without humanity we will become extinct."*

Our current money system is a fiat system built on having no value, every dollar is a counterfeit invention created electronically by a bank and not based on any standard of value. It is worthless paper. The money system is designed to lose value, produce debt and enslave the working class while making a small percentage of humanity wealthy. It is my belief that we can feel there is a great imbalance in our society and to rise above where we are financially at this point may mean we would have to compromise our own integrity. We do not have to compromise our integrity if we only choose to see the good that having more money can do for us.

For example our governments spend more money killing people to get at their resources in wars than it does empowering people to educate them on how to ethically attain money or how to grow crops to feed themselves.

Some Corporations sell products that harm the human body with toxic chemicals or become obsolete just to make bigger profit margins all the while they oppress their employees and give huge bonuses to their CEO's.

Our educational system removed money management from the curriculum in the 1950's which now has most of the population surrendering there money to those who understand its workings better than they do. If you completely understood the way our monetary system worked students would not likely go into debt to have an education for a job that will never give them the financial benefit they would need to repay the loans.

As you can see we have so many mixed emotions and knowledge around this one fear it is hard to find clarity and peace around the topic of money and poverty.

In our Money101 workshops we teach people how to manage one dollar and how to make that dollar grow just by changing the person's perspective from 'Poverty Consciousness' to 'Prosperity Consciousness'. It is just forming a new habit you have never been taught before and it works. The essence of the workshop is to teach the number one 'Rule of Gold', **"Pay yourself first!"**.

We have seen this create life changing habits in individuals without having to get a new job, win a lottery or steal from someone else. Manage what you have, change your focus and money will always find you. You can find more wealth in doing what you love and not causing harm to other people or our environment.

If this were taught in schools there would be no fear of poverty in our society today.

An OVER simplified look at our money system will empower you to begin saving and benefiting from what you currently have to change your money consciousness.

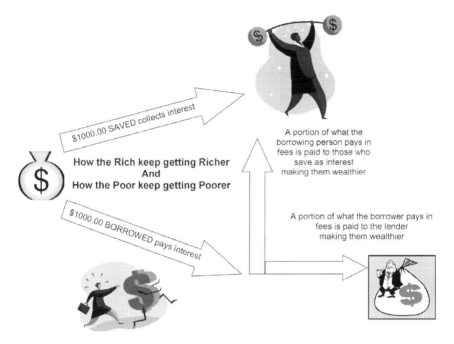

$1000.00 SAVED collects interest

**How the Rich keep getting Richer
And
How the Poor keep getting Poorer**

$1000.00 BORROWED pays interest

A portion of what the borrowing person pays in fees is paid to those who save as interest making them wealthier

A portion of what the borrower pays in fees is paid to the lender making them wealthier

Changing from a Poverty Consciousness to a
Prosperity Consciousness

Developing a money management system that will bring you out of debt is key in overcoming the fear of poverty. To this point I suggest people read the book by George Clason entitled 'The Richest Man In Babylon'

"Learning was of two kinds: the one being the things we learned and knew, and the other being the training that taught us how to find out what we did not know?"

— George S. Clason, The Richest Man in Babylon

How you feel around the topic of money is directly proportional to how much of it you attract. When you find yourself feeling negative around the lack of something in your life, be aware of the feeling and choose to think about something that makes you fell at ease. It takes practice and a little bit of time, but I have discovered it is truest way to find your personal wealth.

Root Fear Epilogue

You are probably becoming aware that these root fears become the foundation of our beliefs. Spending long periods of time with these root fears creates more fear and more phobias. The roots grow and spread to encompass more aspects of your life.

You are probably now aware that 'Fear' in many forms is used to create a culture of enslavement, but it does not have to be this way for you. You have the power to change what and how you think.

What you focus on expands and by continually focusing on the root fears you harbor, you actually bring more of what you do not want into your life.

When we learn to dispel these root fears, the other fears and phobias we have fall away like they were never there. Knowledge, understanding and developing supportive beliefs through techniques we will show you here, will have you living a fearless life and overcome the Learned Helplessness you have developed.

Coming up in the next chapter we will take you on a journey through a field study we did in our workshops on alleviating fears. You will notice the Root Fears we used at the time of the study have changed from the ones you just read. It was because of the data we collected and the analysis of that data that we could better refine and understand what the true root fears were and how we can now have a greater impact at helping people overcome all fears.

Chapter Three

The Fear Relief Study

Over my years of working with thousands of people helping them overcome limitation I have learned a lot about the subject of fear. My interest was drawn to this by Napoleon Hill's 1930's 'Law of Success Course' where he described the '6 Scepters of Fear'.

Hill, believed there were 6 root fears which guided and drove our actions and created our limitations. If this were true a person could clear these 6 fears and no longer be afraid to move forward, phobias would go away and they could finally live the life they dreamed of.

The most common theory to rectifying fear is through exposure to the fear substance. If you had a fear of spiders, for example, you would be confronted with your fear by being exposed to spiders. The challenge with this type of fear resolution is that it is emotionally invasive and has no lasting results. Often times it would only create more trauma in the sufferer.

The method we use to clear fear is called Emotional Freedom Technique or EFT as it is commonly referred to. We wanted to know the overall effects on fears across a broad demographic using EFT. *You will learn more about EFT and how to use it later in this book.*

The Human Experiment:

In 2010 we conducted a human experiment in reducing Fear through a series of small EFT workshops. The workshops were open to anyone who had a Fear or Phobia which they wanted empowerment over. The logic behind the experiment was to see if Napoleon Hill's conclusion on the 6 root fears was valid and if it were possible to clear all fears or phobias merely by clearing the root fears.

I had also hoped that if the above were true we could develop a whole new fast-track way to help people resolve Fear and have more success in life.

The Demographic of attendee's were broke up into 4 age groups; <25 years of age, 25-45, 45-65, >65 years of age. Of which the 45-65 year group made up the largest section of 22 candidates, followed by the 25-45 group with 15 attendee's, >65 with 4 attendees and the <25 group with 3 attendee's for a total of 44 people involved in the study.

The six fears we based the EFT experiment on were; the fear of Death, Illness, Old Age, Loss of Love, Poverty and Criticism as presented by Hill in his study course. We also collected data on 11 other common fears and allowed the attendee's to list an additional 19 specific phobias they had challenges with.

The study group was told they were involved in an experiment to see if their fears and phobias could be reduced by only dealing with 6 root fears. The group rated each of the fears and phobias on the Subjective Units of Distress Scale from 0-10. Ten (10), being your genuine fear or uneasiness of that particular topic when you thought of it.

All the data collected from the surveys was performed without individual one-on-one EFT or coaching, this was to be a generalized study to capture any results across a broad spectrum. The Workshop information was scripted to follow a predefined delivery method as not to skew information between workshops.

In regards to the 6 root fears we discovered a reduction of fear in all groups as follows;

1. In the 'Under 25 years of age' group we witnessed 61% had positive results.
2. The 25-45 year group had 94% results in the reduction of fears
3. The 45-65 year old group experienced 78% positive results in the reduction of fear
4. The final group, over the age of 65, experienced 96% positive results in the reduction of fear.

This averaged out to show us that we had an 82% success rate using EFT to reduce Fears in just a few minutes.

Where the data gets interesting is when we started looking at the other 11 fear/phobias we listed and the additional 19 phobias the study group added to their surveys.

Even though the numbers would show that 18% of the combined group had no positive results in reducing the root fears, they all listed reductions in at least one of the other 11 categories plus the added phobias which were particular to them. In total at the workshops we did not have a single person who did not experience some sort of reduction in their fears and/or phobias.

The EFT process was limited to one round of 30 seconds for each of the root fears for a total time of approximately 3 minutes. The percentage reductions listed below are formed from the Total SUD's (Subjective Units of Distress Scale) before the 3 minutes of EFT and reviewed after the technique was performed at a group level. The Totals include all 4 age groups.

Fear Reduction Chart

6 Root Fears→	Death	Illness	Old Age	Loss of Love	Poverty	Criticism
Total SUD's Level Before EFT	211	258	203	230	238	302
Total SUD's Level After EFT	133	157	125	139	137	187
Percentage Reduction after 3 minutes	↓ 47%	↓ 40%	↓ 38%	↓ 40%	↓ 43%	↓ 38%

The other 11 categories of Fears showed these results;

NOTE: These fears were reduced even though EFT was only performed on the original 6 root fears and not the ones listed below.

	Public Speaking	Snakes Reptiles	Spiders Insects	Heights	Dark	Being Alone
Total SUD's Level Before EFT	230	176	152	166	156	171
Total SUD's Level After EFT	164	120	108	121	120	108
Percentage Reduction after 3 minutes	↓ 29%	↓ 32%	↓ 29%	↓ 27%	↓ 23%	↓ 37%

	Doctors Dentists	Food	Flying	People	Success
Total SUD's Level Before EFT	111	76	117	122	134
Total SUD's Level After EFT	70	59	79	82	78
Percentage Reduction after 3 minutes	↓ 27%	↓ 22%	↓ 32%	↓ 33%	↓ 42%

When we have the opportunity to teach and guide an individual through this process, one-on-one, the results are even more outstanding and fears and phobias are, most of the time, completely eliminated.

In checking with some members of the study group 30 days later it was found that their fears had gone down even more and some reported no longer having the fear or phobia they were originally surveyed on.

We could also detect from the data collected a correlation between the reductions in one of the base fears to another particular phobia or fear on the list. In nearly all cases a reduction in the fear of 'Loss of Love' would also see a proportional reduction the Phobia of 'Spiders & Insects' as well as 'Being Alone'.

An interesting side note to this is, we have always been told by media, psychologists and the like that the Fear of Public Speaking is greater in most people than the Fear of Death.

In this study we found that the Fear of Criticism ranked number one, followed by the Fear of Illness, Poverty and tying for fourth place, the fear of Public Speaking and Loss of Love.

Of course this study we performed was not so much a scientific study as it was an experiment in societal fears & phobias.

What this study proved to our team was;

1. EFT works in minutes
2. EFT has long lasting effects
3. Even the vagueness of the delivery method in EFT still produces positive results
4. All Fears and Phobias have an interconnection amongst themselves that can be used to clear emotional trauma in the individual without requiring specific details in regard to their personal emotional trauma.
5. Most importantly there is an interconnection between all Fears and Phobias. This connection would suggest that all fear has a root and all roots have a seed. Just like gardening when we plant the seed in fertile ground, the roots grow. When we nurture the roots the plant grows

In brief, when we are born unto a certain type of emotional environment it is the fertile ground for our Fear seeds to take root. As we grow in life and nurture our fears by validating them through our false beliefs, more fears become evident and phobias sprout from that nurtured ground.

The study was of great benefit to us as you can see. We now had the ability to closely focus on the true base ingredients and roots of all fears. In our new understanding of the chemical process in the body that is produced by our emotions we have found a more simplified way of explaining the techniques we use to overcome fear.

In our next chapter you will be taken on a journey through the body and will learn how **"No thought lives in the body rent free"**

Chapter Four

HOW FEAR EFFECTS YOU ON A CELLULAR LEVEL

There is a duality to all things, a force and counter force. The counter force to Fear is Love. All other emotions are sub-emotions or derivatives of these two base emotions. In the human body our cells are in one of two states, they are either in Growth or in Protectionism which equals death.

When measured it has been found that Fear produces a long slow frequency in the body which does not support the growth of new cells.

Love is a faster higher frequency that has been shown to touch more DNA Helixes enabling healing and growth, not only the growth of the cell but, the growth of the whole physical matter of the body. Our emotions directly affect every cell in our body which affects our entire existence.

Any Fear we have creates stress in the mind and body. Stress has a physiological response in the body by producing hormones and chemicals that put the body in a Fight or Flight mode. To understand this further we must take a closer look at the makeup of this body to fully comprehend why stress can cause this to happen.

We do not often think of ourselves on much more than the image we see in the mirror every morning with all its features. We can see the image with our eyes; we can hear noises around us. We can touch and feel things with our hands. Inside our chest we can take notice of our heart beating and our lungs breathing in and out.

We have been taught by allopathic medicine these are mechanical functions and are predetermined by our DNA whether we are healthy or defective in some manner. I want to take you on an inner journey and enlightened understanding of the microscopic workings of this body we have and why it works the way it does.

Years ago, I had never given my body much consideration; I too thought I was this sum of parts predetermined by my genetics until I read a book by Dr. Bruce Lipton entitled 'The Biology of Belief'. Dr. Lipton is a former medical school professor and research scientist. His studies of experiments performed in the mid 1960's taught him the body was far more than just a machine built of parts doing different tasks. What Dr. Lipton discovered through his research was a radical new thinking around the central Darwinian dogma that DNA and Genes control our cells. What he discovered was that our DNA is controlled by signals from outside of the cell, including the energetic messages coming from our very own positive and negative thoughts.

Through scientific experiments Dr. Lipton was able to take single cells from the same host and alter them by altering the environment they lived in. In short they were able to take stem cells from the same host, place them in different Petri dishes with different environments and transform the Stem cells into muscle, bone and other tissue. According to Genetics and DNA structure this was supposed to be an impossible process, yet here they had successfully altered the cells without altering the DNA or genetics in any way. The only thing altered was the environment in which the cells were placed.

To understand this better we are going to peer into a microscope and look at an individual cell and how it functions.

The Cellular Body

Dr. Lipton introduced me to a new way of looking at my body and life itself with his explanation of 'smart cells'. Long before life began in the womb from a single cell it began in all existence as a single cell. The cell learned that to better survive it needed to form communities of multi cells all working in harmony. These multi cells, over time, have learned that to exist in this physical environment, they must become more. Cells began forming larger and larger communities developing into many of the life forms we have seen in fossils and throughout the ages until we see this multi celled form as our own human body. Our beginnings did not start with a big bang and then there were creatures of all types but instead from the harmony of one cell working in conjunction with other cells to better survive the abundance of their environment. This simple yet scientifically explainable hypothesis is proving our existence was not dependant on the survival of the fittest but instead survival based on harmonious actions.

Our very survival today is dependant on how well we multi-celled humans learn to be in harmony with all the communities of the planet, and the planet itself or we too will die out leaving once again new patterns of multi-celled creatures to be formed.

Your body is made up of nearly 75 trillion cells (75,000,000,000,000). To grasp the size of that number, if you stacked 75 trillion pennies on top of each other they would reach 59,185,606 miles into outer space, or reach from here to Mars and nearly all the way back.

Each cell is a living microscopic organism made up of nearly 70,000 proteins and amino acids and can contain over 10 Billion molecules.

In just one square centimeter of skin there are no less than 4 million cells. That small community can have sensory and skin cells, blood and capillary cells, hair, follicle, fat, nerve, oil and sweat gland cells. Each one of those cells is performing a particular function that you are not even aware of with your naked eye.

Let's magnify even deeper until we can see only one cell. In this cut-away of a cell we can see there is far more complexity than we could imagine. The cell itself is like our bodies made up of individual mechanisms performing a specific function.

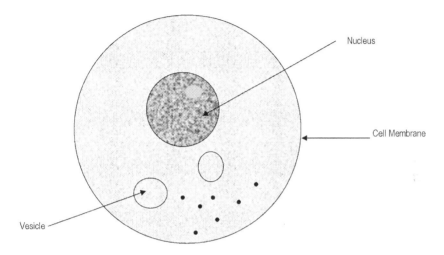

Simple Image of a Human Cell

The inner workings of the cell show a nucleus which is more of an engine than a brain containing the library of our DNA. The outer surface of the cell, the cell membrane, is porous to a degree. Think of it as keyed doorways that will only allow certain proteins and amino acids to enter inside the cell.

***Cell Membrane** is found in all cells. It: 1) separates the inner parts of the cell from the outer environment; and 2) acts as a selectively permeable barrier to allow certain chemicals, namely water, to pass and others to not pass.—From the online Biology Book*

The cell is constantly monitoring its environment outside of itself watching for viruses, toxins and energetic changes. Depending on the environment it senses, it will either produce vaccination chemicals to kill the virus/toxin or if it is hungry, so to speak, it will allow proteins in for fuel. Spent fuel is passed out through the cells as waste. Each living cell is capable of eating, storing energy, defecating, reproducing and most importantly monitoring the environment around the cell itself and reacting to any changes.

Each cell can reproduce through the process of Mitosis, where the cell replicates itself and then separates into two different cells, the old and the new cell. The two cells live in harmony until the host cell dies. In a growth period, of body repair, Mitosis happens at an accelerated rate producing more living cells than dieing cells. The same holds true in cancerous cells, the cells reproduce at accelerated rates forming tumors. Cancer is not a defective disease as much as it is a defective conscious environment which encourages the cells to grow at accelerated rates.

Individual cells build communities of blood cells or muscle and bone cells, skin cells and brain cells. Each cell is a member of a community with a specific function. Each one of those communities makes up the organs, as we have come to call them, which make up the whole of our body. Each cell and each community are working in harmony with the other to make up who you are.

There are no wires tying each cell in the body together, instead the cell depends on wireless communication through the invisible energy field of the body. The energy field itself does not follow nerve canals it flows freely and throughout the whole body. It has even been shown, through scientific experiments, to flow out of and in to the body.

What amazes me is pondering the fact that the energy system causes millions and millions of molecules to come together to form a living cell. Imagine if you will, taking millions of a child's building blocks and pouring them on the floor and then watching as they start to move and organize themselves into shapes and a living existence through no manipulation or intervention of any physical means. The consciousness of the energy field is what is organizing the molecules into the living cells that they will become. We must ask the question, "What is controlling this energy field?"

We must come to the conclusion that the energy field is consciousness in itself and that all life begins with thought, a plan to pattern and create molecules into an organism, the cell, which is the beginning of all life itself. I believe this consciousness to be God-Source, not like the religious humanized God Being we have been taught to believe in but instead a Source of thinking feeling energy which runs through all matter and things even through the subatomic atoms and molecules which are the building blocks of every single cell. These cells combine together make up the whole of the human body and living things around us.

The Merriam Webster Dictionary defines consciousness as;

Definition of CONSCIOUSNESS
1
a: the quality or state of being aware especially of something within oneself
b: the state or fact of being conscious of an external object, state, or fact
c: awareness;

All life begins in the God-Source energy of Consciousness or Thought. The energy field itself THINKS and FEELS! The mere fact that you, as a person, exists was first proposed by a thought or intention of the energy field.

The energy system that the cells monitor and which makes up your consciousness is the very same energy system that is throughout the whole universe running through every galaxy, solar system, planet, rock, plant and animal. When I think of our 'God Source' energy I am reminded of "Intelligent Design". Not in the way it is presented through our religious culture today but instead through the energy environment creatively designing patterns of cells which make up every thing in our universe. It is not disconnected from us; it flows through us and all things.

Our subconscious is also directly connected and part of that great Conscious energy field. Our Conscious 'thinking' ego is what creates the 'disconnect' between our subconscious self and the God-Source.

Our Ego Consciousness is the thought of who we think we are and how we interpret our surroundings from our senses. We are only in harmony with the original God-Source intention which brought us into being who we are, when we feel happy and loved. This is where our healing power comes from.

Our Thoughts produce our feelings; our feelings connect us with the creative energy field of the universe to give us our results . . . Interpretively Good or Bad!

When we do not feel happy and loved we are out of harmony with the energy field such as when we perceive a threat, then the message is spread to every cell of the body and they prepare for a negative reaction. It is in believing that we are limited by our ego thinking consciousness and the sum of our perceptive beliefs that triggers chemical responses in the body and keeps us from healing.

Cell reproduction is shut down and the cells are now in a defensive mode not allowing fuel in or waste out. Every resource within the cell is taxed to its limit.

If we perceive the threat has passed or has subsided somewhat the message is spread throughout the communities of cells in the body and normal operations will begin again.

When we are happy or feeling loved it is like a full on growth cycle because there is no perceived threat to cells, we are tapped into the creative love and growth our bodies desire.

Every FEELING Thought you have changes this cycle in the body so it is important to be stress free. When we are in harmony, feeling good, we are in alignment with original intention of 'who' we came here to be. No thought lives in the body rent free. Physiologically this plays out as follows;

The Fight or Flight Response—When you trigger the fight-or-flight response in your body, it's the equivalent of a head of state declaring war. When war is declared, every industrial resource of a nation is suddenly shifted to the production of munitions. Troops are mobilized, and young people are drafted. The communications and transportation systems of the country are put under military control. Borders are sealed, and security is tightened everywhere. Every one of the country's systems is put on a war footing.

The Fight or Flight explanation – In the body fear and stress are rehearsed in the brain. We do not need to be in an actual stressful event, just thinking about it or reliving it has the same effect. The mobilization in the body causes your immune system to become depressed, as are your digestive and reproductive capabilities. As much as 80% of the blood in your frontal lobes drains out to feed your muscles, which is why sages have told us for hundreds of years to never make any decisions while you're upset.

Studies are revealing, Fight or Flight is not triggered only by major fearful events, like an animal attack. Consider the married couple who have an argument, get angry and frustrated, and then withdraw into frustrated silence. The argument represents FIGHT, and silence or sarcastic rejection represents FLIGHT.

Researchers Study Energy Psychology – In a study published in Counseling and Clinical Psychology Journal, psychologist Jack Rowe, PhD

There are many different hormones produced in the body and brain which are used as signals to the rest of the cells in the body. Many of these hormones are present at all times within the body and are ready to be called upon in a moments notice by the energy field of the body.

During moments of stress, the Hypothalamus in the brain produces Cortisol and other hormones like Norepinephrine. When you are relieved of stress you brain switches to natural healing hormones like Endorphins and Serotonin.

High level or prolonged high levels of Cortisol can cause;

➢ Cell reproduction to be altered and nearly shut down.
➢ Reduced elasticity in the Skin
➢ Reduced muscle mass
➢ Reduced Bone Density
➢ Heart rate, blood pressure and blood sugars are increased as the large muscle groups prepare to either Fight or Flee.
➢ Can damage the immune system, which explains why we catch more colds when we are stressed. It may intensify symptoms in diseases that have an autoimmune component, such as rheumatoid arthritis. It also seems to affect headaches and irritable bowel syndrome, and there are now suggestions of links between stress and cancer.
➢ Blood is drawn in from the extremities like the hands and feet and shunted to the larger muscle groups. Hand/foot temperature ranges over 40° degrees from a low of 60° degrees to as high as 99° degrees F. Changes of 5° degrees or more can take place in seconds.
  o Below 79 degrees—Chronic Tension
  o 79-84 degrees—Slight Tense
  o 84-90 degrees—Nervous
  o 90-95 degrees—Calm
  o Above 95 degrees F—Deeply Relaxed
➢ In the brain parts of the frontal cortex are shut down which diminishes your reasoning capability. In stressful situations we lack the reasoning capability we need to make rational

decisions. Have you ever been in an argument with someone and later thought of all the things you should have or could have said?

➢ Reduced memory and learning
➢ Reduced neuron growth which is required to turn short term memory into long term memory

Source: Dr. Dawson Church—Study of Cortisol Effects on the Body

The link between stress and heart disease is well-established. If stress is intense, and stress hormones are not 'used up' by physical activity, our raised heart rate and high blood pressure put tension on arteries and cause damage to them. As the body heals this damage, artery walls scar and thicken, which can reduce the supply of blood and oxygen to the heart. This is where a fight-or-flight response can become lethal: Stress hormones accelerate the heart to increase the blood supply to muscles; however, blood vessels in the heart may have become so narrow that not enough blood reaches the heart to meet these demands. This can cause a heart attack.

Stress is also associated with mental health problems and, in particular, anxiety and depression. Here the relationship is fairly clear: the negative thinking that is associated with stress also contributes to these

Chronic stress and being in a state of high Cortisol for prolonged periods also has another interesting effect. It begins to deteriorate or erode the Hypothalamus stem in the brain. The Hypothalamus interprets this as a need to produce more Cortisol. It becomes an addiction for the Hypothalamus. The cells also become addicted to the constant stream of Cortisol, so messages are sent throughout to the body to repeat what is was doing to produce more stress so that more Cortisol can be produced.

This last point is an important one to understand and comprehend. When we are emotionally in a state of constant or chronic fear and stress the body develops an addiction for the drug the cells now want, which is Cortisol. When a person tries to change their life to overcome their fear or stress they always seem to get drawn back in to repeat behaviors.

For example, a person is in an emotionally abusive relationship when they decide to break free. Things are great for a while and then they choose another partner and very soon they find themselves back in another emotionally or physically abusive relationship. You might wonder why we keep getting the same results.

Or,

The person who is trying to change from living in poverty to attain more wealth only to find that something always comes up or disrupts their life and everything comes unraveled again. It seems like a vicious cycle. You often hear the phrase, *"The rich keep getting richer and the poor keep getting poorer"*.

From all the scientific studies done on cellular biology I believe the answer lies in understanding the addictive process of the cells and how stress experienced from emotional distress creates these chemical addictions. Understanding this helps us to understand our behavioral patterns.

The second point to understand is the energy field which runs through our body runs through all things, even others, and our bodies can energetically sense in others the ability to fulfill the cellular chemical addiction.

The longer we spend in these addictive stressed states the harder it can be for the cells to reprogram themselves. You would think that during Mitosis of new cells this addiction may not be there but you need to see these two cells live together as one for a short period of time where the host cell passes on information to the new cell.

On a larger scale the same holds true within the mother's womb. The emotional environment created within the mother becomes a learned behavior in the new child. In those early years the new person is absorbing information about the environment and learning how to react in it to survive. The problem with this lies in the negative environment around those early learning years. This sets up chemical addictions within the cells of the new person and can cause dis-ease and the need to be in similar stressful situations. Behavioral patterns in parents can often be found in their children although most people do not like to hear they are just like one of their parents.

Just as these programs can be placed in people they can also be changed or reprogrammed through developing a new paradigm using the tools we will be teaching you later in this book.

All cells in the body have a life cycle, some are replaced daily and others are replaced over years. As an example the cells in your stomach lining and intestines are replaced every 3-4 days. Billions of cells are evacuated from the body through your digestive tract every 72 hours. During this process of Mitosis and change within the cells the information passed on by the host cell can be changed.

To change a program within a cell it would take a few life cycles of changing the energy environment (our feeling thoughts) within the body.

To relate to this, think for a moment of the father laying on his death bed, his son standing beside him. The father wants to pass his wisdom on to his son so he can better survive in the world.

The fathers says, *"Son we live in a toxic place filled with enemies and people who would do us wrong. So you need to become a soldier and fight the insurgence. Never give up!"*

Now the environment changes and the story changes;

When it comes time for that son who is now the father to pass on his information to his son he says, *"Son, we live in a toxic environment, no wait it used to be a toxic environment. And there are enemies all around us, no wait, that's not true either. You need to become a aaaahhhhh . . ."* and the father dies before he can finish his message.

The son must now determine from the environment what he must become. It will not likely be a soldier when there is no threat.

This simplified scenario is played out in the cells in each mitosis. How you FEEL determines the environment the cells need to live in. If it is toxic, with negative energy and toxic chemicals from the foods we consume, the cells will design themselves from their DNA library how to best survive in that environment.

Your Fears form your beliefs and produce stress in your body on a cellular level.

The good news is, when you have feeling thoughts of love and forgiveness different hormones and chemicals are produced in the body.

Serotonin and Endorphins are what I like to call the 'Happy Hormones'. They;

- ➢ Promote cellular regeneration
- ➢ Strengthen the Autoimmune system
- ➢ Improve your mood
- ➢ Increase energy
- ➢ Make you feel happy
- ➢ Help you sleep better
- ➢ Are Natural Pain Killers

To stimulate the production of these chemicals within the body we need to relieve our stress and learn to love and forgive ourselves. In the relief healing begins.

I have often said we do not need to forgive the world or the person who did some monstrous thing to us; we only have to forgive ourselves for believing we are at fault in some way in the process.

Changing your beliefs to live a fearless life can now have your cellular body become addicted to these new chemicals and everything changes. You have probably heard it said, *"The better it gets, the better it gets".* Or, *"That person is so lucky they seem to have the Midas touch".*

DNA Change and Intention *– An ingenious HeartMath experiment used human placenta DNA to determine whether the DNA could be altered by intentions of anger, appreciation and love. The research found that an energetic connection exists between structures in the quantum vacuum and corresponding structures on the physical plain, and that this connection can be influenced by human intentionality.*

The challenge in changing our habits is becoming truly conscious of what our habits are. For example a person who speeds is likely to speed all the time and justify in their mind that what they are doing is OK. The person who eats a particularly unhealthy food will justify their actions by stating they need to have it.

The program running in our sub consciousness can have us believing we are justified in its very being. The chemical keyways have been set in place and change to those patterns can often be interpreted by the cellular body as a threat.

Understanding the programs and learning how to change them is the next chapter in our journey . . . .

Chapter Five

YOUR ACTIONS SPEAK LOUDER THAN WORDS

There are so many things we want to change in our lives but feel utterly useless that we cannot change. The feeling of Self-Doubt or low Self-worth, is the very thing that keeps us from getting the things we want.

By now you should begin to realize that our feeling thoughts are what create our current circumstances good or bad. Many of you would argue, *"I never asked for this to happen to me."* You would be correct, you never out-and-out asked for it but your subconscious thoughts are a recipe of feelings.

When I say 'Feeling Thoughts' I mean these are our true inner truths that show us a result. Your subconscious energy field which feeds all cells in your body is only monitoring feelings and thoughts. The cells in your body do not know any difference between a good thought or a bad thought, they just react to the conscious energy field you have within you.

Thoughts come from the conscious brain and are solely a byproduct of your perception of yourself and the world around you. Many of your feeling thoughts are not supportive of who you truly are but each one good or bad sets up a feeling within you which gives you a result. These thoughts have become the internal programs you are running and appear to be hard to change.

Think of your conscious self as the calculator trying to change the programs in the computer (Subconscious). You can press all the buttons you want, wish upon a star, pray to God or sell your soul and it will not make a bit of difference because you are not speaking in the language of the subconscious energy field which is emotional energy.

You cannot simply wish for more money, you must first understand how more money would make you feel.

You cannot wish for the new romance in your life you first must feel what that would genuinely feel like for you.

You cannot wish to be a healthier person you must feel what it would be like to be healthy.

In those three scenarios we may have no clue of what it is like to have any of those things. Perhaps there is no family history or you have never experienced those feelings before. It is hard to form a new feeling-thought with something you have no experience with.

Now the question becomes 'How' do we change our chemical programs with feelings when we have no clue of what they feel like. The answer is in letting go of the resistive thoughts and feelings and finding peace and love within yourself.

Here is where the science gets really interesting, when we alleviate our fears and find comfort in our new thoughts the emotional feelings are already there. That place of inner peace IS the solution to changing everything which you have perceived and understand you are the one who has written your life story and it is you who can change it by simply feeling better about yourself. It is in the 'knowing' that you are worthy and deserving of all your desires where the powerful ability to change begins.

As you read the following stories listen for the 'knowing' which each story plays out.

Emotional Example One – Why the Rich get Richer

Scenario 1: Born into a family of means John has never felt nor realized what it is like to be poor. There is no fear of poverty because the family has never known poverty. John can only see the abundance in his world and his ability to capitalize from it. The energy field within John only knows how to attract more abundance to him. Remember the energy field not only runs through us but through every living thing. Without feelings of poverty the Natural way of being is through abundance. There is no shortage of money or resources currently in the world, only a shortage of people that know what it feels like to have all that stuff at your finger tips. It is not unlike an elitist way of thinking and feeling. John <u>knows</u> what it is like to be able to first want something and then get the money to buy into his dreams.

The poor to John are not people who can't get their own riches, they are people who do not want to learn how to get their own riches. To John the poor are lazy, thieves and beggars who are not willing to put enough effort into life that is why they deserve to be servants of the wealthy.

Scenario 2: Jack born into a world of poverty has to struggle for every penny. He has watched his parents do the same and their parents before them were also poor. The rich, to Jack, are corrupt and evil they never do anything nice for anyone. To Jack, rich people are lazy thieves and con-artists preying off the weak and poor. The rich should be brought to there knees for what they have done to Jack. There is lots of blame to go around of why he cannot get his share of the wealth. To Jack it is the governments fault, his parents fault, the wealthy are out to get him, he has to work hard for every dollar while rich people are all lazy and everything comes handed to them on a silver plate. Jack is a victim of society and someone else should pay his way, he is entitled to that. Every emotion around energy within Jack is a corrupt one, and one that is out of harmony with the abundance that is all around him. The same opportunities that are available to the wealthy are also available to the poor the only difference is their perception and their ability to react in those situations. Jack has had many million dollar ideas but someone else always seems to beat him to it.

Can you see the patterns in the two different perceptions around money? It is hard to attain something you hate so much. Even though you wish to have wealth, until you learn how to reprogram those feeling-thoughts you are emotionally and chemically running within your body you will be tied to the same result.

John can only see Jack as being his own worst enemy. Jack can only see John as the reason he cannot get what he wants. They are just two completely different ways of thinking. Neither of the two is evil, their fears and habits are their beliefs hence their programs.

Both people can have fears but the inner programs they have running will have different causal effects in their lives. Both can be unhappy but still the programs do not change. Their lives are a result of what they feel they know.

Donald Trump, born into a family of means, lost millions of dollars only to bounce back within a few years to be worth billions of dollars. A person with a poverty consciousness could not make the same decisions and have the same outcome as Mr. Trump because they have no idea of what the feeling of wealth is.

Families who are entrepreneurial have a tendency of raising their children to do the same. Children are taught how to have money make more money.

Families who are in the service sector tend to have their children follow their footsteps. Children are taught to scrimp and save but many want what the rich have so they go into debt to make themselves feel wealthier.

These are habitual programs which have been taught to run within us since we were in the womb. The child will honor the ways of whichever parent influenced them most through its created desires in life.

To change the habit of 'Poverty Consciousness' one has to begin with "What it would feel like to have those things" and then the management of what you currently have AND, most importantly, be grateful for what you currently have. Even if what you have is not that much.

In most parts of the world just having a roof over your head, food in your stomach and a television is considered being wealthy. That's right, those three things are a consideration of wealth to most of the people on this planet. Having any or all of those things is reason enough to be grateful. Now, look around your home and notice the wealth you already have. Yes, there may be things there that you bought on credit, however, be grateful you had enough credit to even buy those things.

By definition wealth is;.
1. **a.** An abundance of valuable material possessions or resources; riches. *As stated, to many wealth is just owning a TV*
   b. The state of being rich; affluence. *Affluence also means moving toward a point of abundance. Just being on the journey itself*

2. All goods and resources having value in terms of exchange or use. *All aspects of our life have value. One of the greatest wishes of our modern society today is to have 'Wealth of Time' to spend with family and friends*

3. A great amount; a profusion: a wealth of advice. *The Wealth of experience you have gained on your journey counts towards your value in life. Have you been learning and growing?*

Based on the source definition at; TheFreeDictionary.com

When we change our perspective of what wealth is you begin to realize it is something you have already attained on many levels in your life go to that feeling of gratitude and allow yourself to experience in the knowing feeling.

There is a large percentage of the people on our planet who feel it is better to be spiritual than it is to have wealth but as you can see now by the definition of wealth it holds a far greater meaning than just procession of more stuff. Abundance must be a 'Whole-istic' way to view the physical experience we call life. Body, Mind and Spirit are the fundamentals of who we are. It is no more righteous to be spiritual than it is to seek wealth. The cautionary sense of seeking wealth must be one of doing it in harmony with all living things on the planet.

It is my belief there are many ways to be creative to create more wealth for one's self. My simple philosophy is to make sure that what I am charging a fee for should be of value. The products I sell should not be at the cost of our planet and should benefit every person from the creation of the product, to packaging and marketing.

Changing your Current Habit around money would be to change your money management habits. Adopt a habit of saving a percentage of every dollar you make as your own. As you create this habit your consciousness will change and your programs will change

Emotional Example Two – Finding my Soul Mate

Scenario 1:

Judy was raised in a home where her parents were loving and affectionate towards each other and towards her. She was coddled and told how beautiful she was on the inside and the outside. She was enrolled in the programs that would make her a better person. Judy was taught that "Life responds to your outlook" and she had a clear definition of the type of life she wanted. She would dream of her prince charming as having a certain look and he would love and support her for who she was and what she wanted to be. Judy wrote in her diary of the perfect man and described every detail of his being. Later in life Judy met her prince charming and she felt like she knew him her whole life. She met lots of wonderful people in her life and made many good friends who loved to be around her. Judy could not understand why others had such a hard time doing this. Judy thought there must be something wrong with someone else if they could not find their 'soul mate'. "There is someone out there for us all", she would say.

Scenario 2:

Carmen came from a broken home with a father who was an abusive alcoholic and a mother who had no self esteem. Her mother would always side with her father or one of her siblings and never protect her perceptions. As Carmen developed into a young woman her mother would often start fights with her or embarrass her by flirting with the boy friends she brought home. Carmen had her looks and used them to go through many relationships only to find that the men she met were all abusive and worthless. She could find no soul mate so she settled into an unhappy life of being with someone who was, at best, mediocre. He would eventually leave her and she became very bitter towards everyone in her life especially men.

Once again we can see the two different patterns of feeling-thoughts. One of feeling loved and appreciated the other feeling bitter and of low self-worth. Both were beautiful women but from different patterns of learning. Judy was taught to love herself while Carmen was taught to loathe herself.

When Judy was told she was just like her mother she felt honored and blessed to be just like her. When Carmen was told she was like her mother she would get angry and react with great discourse saying, "I am nothing like my $##%(*() mother!".

When you are raised learning how to love yourself finding others to share your love is natural. To find the love in the world the first journey must be in finding the love within your self and the beauty in others. This is one of the most profound discoveries you will make. The feeling of love within yourself can be as subtle as allowing yourself to feel at peace. In 'Peace' you can find the 'Knowing' of what love is.

Emotional Example Three – Healthy People are Born That way

Scenario 1:

Sandra came from a working family, her parents loved her but had fast paced lives of their own where time together was a challenge. Meal time was family time so the family sat down and ate healthy meals together. Her parents were very health conscious, mom used to be on the regional soccer team and her dad nearly made it to the nationals in the football league.

She was taught her body is a temple and to be conscious of what she feeds it and how she treats it.

The family gardened together in the summer time and used the bounty of their garden to fill their nutritional needs and the freezer for the winter.

When the weekends came around the family always did something fun or exciting right after the weekend chores were done. Her mom always helped her with the chores inside the house while her dad always took care of the yard work, something she always took pleasure in on those nicer days. Sandra's parents made sure she was involved in after school sports activities. Soccer, Track & Field and swimming were her favorite sports. They were an active family even though they were a very busy family.

Sandra loved to feel good about herself and eating healthy made sure she never got sick too often.

Scenario 2:

Theresa also came from a working family, her parents loved her too but things were a little different. Meal times were never spent together because they worked different shifts or dad got home at a later time. Meals were sporadic and made with lots of quick and easy processed foods. When Theresa starting showing signs of gaining a little weight her mother instantly put her on a diet and seemed to remind her daily of how fat she was becoming. Her mom thought she was helping Theresa through 'tough love' initiatives.

Dad would comment that she wasn't fat just big boned like his side of the family and not to worry about it.

When Sandra wanted attention she was shoved off into her room or in front of the television. She occupied her time and need for attention with food. The commercials reminded her to eat lots of unhealthy foods. She didn't belong to a sports team so she and her friends used to make fun of all the 'Skinny Bitches' behind their backs.

Scenario 3:

Dave came from a hard working family. They always ate good but because they led very physical lives they ate BIG meals. Dave had eaten like this for many years. When Dave got out of college he noticed he had put on a few pounds but thought he just needed to work out more. Dave continued to eat the same huge portions of food everyday until one day he noticed he was largely overweight.

In all three of these scenarios it was the habits that were created around food and exercise that dictated the outcome. To overcome the last 2 eating disorders, Theresa would have to overcome her eating and exercising habits plus she would also have a challenge of eating out of boredom or out of filling a need for lost love.

Dave on the other hand would likely only have to overcome his meal portion size and possibly some emotional stress challenges he picked up later in life.

Sandra lived many years and was active throughout her life. When she started her family, food and exercise were at the top of her list for her children.

Theresa made lots of excuses for her eating habits like, "I gotta have my chocolate or French fries". She too started a new family, her children were obese by the age of seven. Theresa developed diabetes, kidney problems, sore muscles and joints from the atrophy of not being used enough and poor nutrition. She tried many different weight loss programs and none of them worked on her because she believed, "My metabolism is different than other people who can lose weight easily".

It is the habits we create in the cellular body that make us crave for more of what we do not need. Fat cells are really just cells which have huge stores of fat within them. Teach the cells that the emotional environment is a healthy one, give the cells the proper fuel they were designed to run on and they will lose their fat content knowing the threat has passed. Feeding your body a daily dose of 'Love' and 'Forgiveness' to each and every cell is the beginning of changing the way you currently are. There are no incurable situations or diseases, just unchanging beliefs and perceptions in your heart.

There is so much information around diet and lifestyle it would take the rest of this book to entertain a program that is right for you. In my experience of suffering from poor health and then regaining my health I have discovered a very simple philosophy that works for me and when taught to others it has changed their health permanently.

That simple philosophy follows the elemental characteristics of age old cultures and then adapted to our society today. It begins with loving the food you are putting in your body and know that it is the fuel your body needs to become healthy.

In simplicity, food should be natural and from nature not processed by man and altered to have no nutrients.

Daily exercise should stimulate every cell in your body and reward each cell with nutrition and the life supporting elements which each one needs. Exercising does not need to be hard it only requires the stimulation of circulation to each cell in your body.

On the next page I will guide you through my simple philosophy for better health.

Since the beginning of recorded history in all cultures we have followed four basic elements of life they are: Earth, Wind, Fire, and Water. How I adapted this to my lifestyle was to create some simple rules I could follow.

Earth:
If it is grown in rich soil and nurtured without the use of chemicals I will eat it. Our bodies were designed to operate best on a diet based largely on plant food and very little on animal protein. It is the life in the plants themselves which feed and fuel our bodies on a cellular level. The more chemicals and processing involved in getting food to your table the less life and more toxins you are consuming which is not the food cells need to be healthy and grow.
Wind:
I have reinterpreted this to equal Breath. Spending 10-15 minutes every day slowing your breathing down and taking deep long breaths has been proven to energize every cell in your body. It is another element all cells need to survive and be healthy. Exercise should also involve deep breathing. Breathing combined with simple stretching exercises move toxins and large proteins out the cells through the Lymphatic system.
Fire:
This I have reinterpreted to equal Light. Of all the things our bodies need sunshine is a key element for the production and maintenance of Vitamin 'D' in our body, the very building block of our immune system. If you live in an area where you do not get at least 20 minutes of sunlight to 40% of your body every day then you will need to supplement with large doses of Vitamin 'D' the sunshine vitamin. The energy our cells derive from the sun can be likened to being solar powered. Exercise also produces heat in the body which stimulates our natural ability to fight off infections.
Water:
The last of the four most important elements our cellular bodies need is water. There are lots of theories around how much we should drink and should we include soda, coffee, milks and other drinks in with that. To me water by itself is already in its purest form why add anything else to it like sugar, caffeine, dairy fat or chemicals we do not need.

For more information on the **'Healthy Elemental Lifestyle'** visit our website at www.GiveUpPain.com

*   *   *

The three examples discussed in this chapter are not to depict that life is exactly like that in your particular case. These were 3 very black and white scenarios we played out for you. Of course there are hundreds of different ways to be raised, the conditioning we get in those early years is what defines our patterns later on. It is not that you are defective in any way or it is your FATE. It is only your perception and what you are willing to do to change those perceptions so that you may experience all the good things life has to offer you. You are worthy of your desires!

Habits are programs in your body. Whether or not it is a physical habit, a mental habit or a spiritual habit, it can be changed once you identify the source and come to the realization that you can change it.

Time Does Not Heal All Emotional Wounds – The Center of Disease Control conducted a study of 17,421 people over a five year period. The study showed a strong inverse link between emotional well-being, health, and longevity on the one hand, and early life stress on the other like children who grew up in emotionally toxic environments. It emphasizes that there are some negative experiences that we just don't "get over", and that TIME DOES NOT HEAL.

Time may not heal all wounds but you have a choice on how your perceive your life and then change that by letting go of old non-supportive beliefs and perceptions.

Changing of the Guard

The Success Formula we discussed in the beginning of this book shows us to first change, we need a desire to change (LoD). Secondly we need to identify the Current Habit (CH) and change that.

If you are unhappy with your life journey so far, then I would say it is time to make some changes. Your Level of Desire must be able to overcome the comfort zone, even though it seems uncomfortable, of your Current Habits. The only thing standing in the way of you changing your level of desire or your current habits is your current belief about who you are. Who you believe you are was formed from false perceptions handed down to you from others.

Your journey of habit change begins with 'Baby Steps'. A philosopher stated, *"There are only two ways to change a current habit. The first is through a 'traumatic emotional event'. The second is through 'constant speech repetition'."*

A 'traumatic emotional event' would be like having a health scare large enough to have you insist on change and use your new found 'desire to live' to change what is out of whack. In essence you become 'Sick-and-tired' of being literally sick and tired. The person living in poverty or the person who has lost everything because of their money management skills finally decides enough is enough and fervently begins to work with passion to never be that way again. This is the 'forced' way out of our Learned Helplessness. We do not necessarily deal and resolve the emotional programs that put us in those positions in the first place. What can happen, if the emotional aspect is not dealt with, the programs at some point can repeat themselves after the burst of desire has subsided.

In the case of 'constant speech repetition', you would be asked to use positive affirmations to change your life. This works for many who do not have he deep roots of fear and emotional trauma which is developed over time. The challenge with this process is it can take years and years of affirmations to change your perspective and depending on the programs you have running it may never work for you.

Step One in the changing of the guard, those old thought patterns, must be to first understand how you got them and then learn how to discount their validity. Until this process takes place all the positive affirmations in the world will simply not work. The reason for this is plain and simple, you cannot say something positive to yourself without having your inner voice whisper back, "Bull Shit".

The negative emotional state you have developed through your root fears must first be negated so there is no emotional reaction to a positive statement other than a feeling of openness. Openness is the lack of internal emotional resistance we build around our beliefs.

A friend came to see me a few years back with some financial challenges. They wanted change in their life because they were tired of the constant financial crisis they were always in. It appeared that they would build up their income and then an emergency would happen and they would lose everything. They obviously had the Desire to change but didn't think that it could possibly be any emotional event from their past which was holding them back. This person had been using positive affirmations for over eight years with no success and no apparent changes in their lifestyle. Things remained the same. I challenged them to try this new technique I had discovered to alleviate their past emotional trauma. They were very reluctant because they thought they would have to relive those traumatic events over again as other therapies did. After explaining that they were already reliving those events emotionally every day anyway they decided to try our technique. With this technique you will learn later in this book, there is no need to relive or tell your inner most secrets to anyone. After less than 15 minutes they were able to replay those emotional events in their life, of which I knew no details, without any emotional connection. They were astonished at the simplicity and a little embarrassed because they had waited for so long to resolve these issues. Today, their financial crisis is no longer a challenge. The positive affirmations, which they continued to do, are now having the positive effect they were supposed to have.

When we change the root of the program to have no emotional effect on us anymore the environment within the cellular community's changes and you begin to attract to you through the energy field those things you thought you could not do or have. Every living thing in this physical world is connected through the same energy field and when we are in a state of allowing things to come to us it happens.

When fear and emotional upset are relieved, stress is relieved. When stress is relieved it is like hitting the record button on a tape recorder. We are now open to change our lives in any manner we choose by using 'constant speech repetition' and 'feeling thoughts' to change the internal programs we have running.

The actions we now take have lasting positive results and are now louder than the old 'feeling thoughts' we had going on.

In our next chapter we going to begin scoring our fears and recognizing the programs we have running through a very simple process.

This process is the starting point to recognizing and understanding how these fears are keeping you from that which you desire.

Chapter Six

FINDING YOUR INNER TRUTHS

We often think we know who we are has been decided already by fate or a divine plan which is guiding our life. We feel we are victims of circumstances beyond our own control and resolve to live a life of mediocrity. The challenge with that thinking is we never strive to grow and become more. We never strive to find harmony in our world and our true intention of why we came to this physical plain.

We all have the ability to become more, not better than any other person, just more than what we currently are. Every person on this planet is at a different emotional level than the other.

Some are young and inquisitive growing and seeking knowledge while others feel they are victims and choose to give in to their circumstances. They have surrendered to their beliefs and programs.

One thing is definite we all have an internal struggle going on with our emotions. How we perceive our world becomes our beliefs. Even slight changes to our perception can have monumental results.

In my lifelong study of people there is a sense that we need to be perfect and we need to defend our beliefs. If our beliefs were wrong, we would be wrong and further away from the perfection we feel we must be. The truth of the matter, there is no person on this planet that is perfect in their beliefs nor is there a need to ever think we must be perfect. Perfection is an unattainable hunger which can never be satisfied. If instead we looked at our lives and realized, as humans, we all make mistakes, we all have emotional events which infect our minds daily. Perhaps our new belief should be, "I am becoming more. I am learning. I am perfecting my skills."

Perfecting feels better than perfection. Becoming more feels differently than "Being better than other people". This arrogance of being better than others and holding your beliefs as perfection is a false premise to build your life on and it usually only creates internal emotional strife that will needlessly be suffered.

Every time we have a need to be 'right' we are judging our beliefs as being better than the other persons. If we listened to another person perceptive on any given topic, with an open mind, we would learn that reasoning and comprehension are three dimensional aspects of our mind and not two dimensional, black or white situations.

We could give you any topic at this moment and discover that because of past experiences you could learn from another's perspective. The perspective you have locked yourself into is the very corner stone of your beliefs which is preventing you from growing and becoming more.

Psychology becomes Physiology *– What we believe about ourselves alters our reality. A 2007 Harvard study examined the difference between physical exertion and physical exertion plus belief. The researchers recruited 84 maids who cleaned hotel rooms. The sample was divided into 2 groups. One group heard a brief presentation explaining that their work qualifies as good exercise. The other group did not. Over the next 30 days the women that received the exercise presentation lost an average of 2 pounds, lowered their blood pressure by almost 10%, and displayed drops in body fat percentage, Body mass index, and waist-to-hip ratio.*

These corner stone beliefs are the programs we have running in our subconscious. Once the subconscious programs have been formed the difficulty lies in changing them. According to psychology the only way to change a belief system is either through constant speech repetition or a Traumatic Emotional Event. I am sure most people would sooner change their belief programs before they hit rock bottom than to actually wait for rock bottom to hit them. That being said, we need to understand how these programs are formed, why you are running them and then become consciously aware of when you are running them. It is in the awareness of the belief where we can consciously choose a different thought and rewrite the program.

How and Why Programs are formed;

You have become a product of your subconscious programs. The programs run unattended within us from beliefs we have formed from our past experiences.

I turn to the teachings of Dr. Bruce Lipton to explain how these programs are formed. As I listened to Dr. Lipton explain this to me it all made so much sense. Often the deepest of understandings can come from the simplest of explanations. The following is paraphrased from Dr. Lipton;

Remember the first time you drove a car? As you sped up you felt anxious and thought of how fast it seemed you were going. You concentrated on each movement and observed the rush of information coming at you like road signs, traffic lights, and other vehicles swerving in and out. It was almost overwhelming at the time. Your fear felt like it was in the back of your throat. The tension you felt in your hands and fingers' tightly gripping the steering wheel was nearly painful. Each of those first experiences driving a car were harrowing to say the least.

However, when we consciously learn how to drive a car, it is not very long before we are driving down the road talking on the phone, drinking a coffee and singing along with the radio as if there was nothing to fear. The question then becomes "Who is driving the car?"

Was it the fearful person who started out driving or was it a program in your subconscious mind that is driving the car.

The subconscious is the Central Voice of the body that commands unison and harmony from the trillions of cells of the body. It is the central voice that acquires and learns the perceptions that we must deal with throughout our lives. The purpose of forming these subconscious programs is to free the conscious mind to learn more. Imagine what it would be like if you had to consciously think to breath, make your heartbeat or even chew your food. The Conscious thinking mind which is much less powerful than the Subconscious Central voice would be overwhelmed and you would not be able to function. As we develop and build these programs the body builds cellular memory which effectively takes over the task for the conscious mind.

If a program of fear is running how we deal with a particular situation then the body is commanded by the Central Voice on how to react. Changing the program is the difficult task or so it would seem.

To change a program we must once again become conscious of the task of training the body how to handle a particular emotional series of events.

From our last chapter we learned some modern thinking has us believing that if we shout positive affirmations at the programs this will change the program and thereby we will be healed.

In the vast majority of cases it is not the shouting at the TV set to change to a different show that changes the channel, it is the conscious effort of picking up the remote and pressing a button that actually performs the task and now we can watch a new program.

In this over simplified explanation lays a clue for us on how to change our programming. It is conscious feeling and thinking effort that must be applied.

The subconscious awareness is a million times more powerful than the conscious awareness. The person yelling at themselves in the mirror, "I want to be a millionaire" is not going to change their current condition. The subconscious voice is ignoring the conscious voice waiting for the reprogramming. What changes the programming is, letting go of the fear based belief's around money, becoming aware of when your fear program is being activated and consciously learning how to manage your money.

All programs can be changed and altered so you can live a happier, healthier, more prosperous life.

"True healing of the body and soul comes when we learn to speak the truth to ourselves."

To find out your inner feeling thoughts we must now take a journey in finding out "Who I Am". Identifying your inner truth is revealed in our "I am" statements. Listen to the language you use on a daily basis. The vocabulary we use is based on the fearful inner programs our subconscious is running.

For Example;

When someone tells you, you look good, how do you respond?

Do you say *"Thank You"* and think, *"Wow, is that person ever perceptive and nice"* or, do think *"What do they want, I do not look good today. My hair is a mess, I look like crap, I am fat, blah, blah, blah"*.

Ask this of yourself; look in the mirror, tell yourself you look good and listen to the inner voice whispering back comments to you. Write down your answer(s) and keep them hidden out-of-sight where nobody can find them until we teach you our newest technique for clearing those negative programs.

When a close friend asks you to go on a trip with them and it will only cost a couple of thousand dollars. Do you cringe inside and say *"I can't afford to go"* or do you feel you must lie to get out of this embarrassing situation, *"Oh I can't go, I am way too busy"*.

What do you think of your personal financial situation at this very point if someone asked you that question?

Do you feel like you have failed somewhere along the way?

Write down your response and hang on to it until we take you through the 'clearing the program' exercises later in this book.

For this next exercise you will need a piece of paper or a notebook and a pen or pencil. Go get those things right now and Write down your responses for these questions;

1. Do you feel loved in your current relationships with your partner, family and friends?

    a. Is there something wrong with them, if so What is it?

2. Is you mother a negative influence on your life?

    a. If Yes, Why do feel that is true?

3. Is your father a negative influence on your life?

    a. If so, How do you feel about him?

4. Do you honestly love yourself?

    a. If not, What do you feel is wrong with you?

5. Do you feel alone or empty inside?

    a. Why do you feel the way you do on this topic?

6. Do you feel stupid when it comes to life challenges?

    a. Why do you think that is?

7. Do you have many friends?

    a. If not, why do you think that is?

8. Do you see the good in others and not yourself?

    a. What do you see wrong in other people?

9. Can you accept yourself for the way you are at this very moment?

    a. What one small thing could you do to change that?

10. Are you angry with yourself?

    a. For what reason?

11. Are you angry with someone in your life past or presently?

    a. If yes, Why and for What reason?

12. Can you forgive others that have transgressed against you?

    a. If not, Why?

13. Do you love animals more than you love other people?

    a. If so, Why?

14. What is your opinion of what is wrong with our world today?

    a. Is there some person who is at fault?

15. Do you like helping other people?

    a. Why?

16. Have you ever had a time of need and had to ask for help from someone else?

    a. How did that make you feel?

17. Do you blame others for the way you currently are?

    a. If so, How do you think they have affected you?

18. Are you happy with the person you are in a relationship with currently?

    a. Do they remind of you of anyone else you may know?

19. Do you forgive yourself for all the bad things you have done? Spend some time thinking back as far as you can and see if there are any guilty moments or feelings within you.

20. Are you afraid of creatures, animals or darkness?

21. Who are you afraid of most?

    a. Why are you afraid of them?

22. Have you ever failed at something that was important to you in your life?

    a. What did you fail at?
    b. Why do you think you failed?

23. Do you take care of your physical health with proper nutrition and exercise?

    a. If not, Why do think that is?

24. Are you in any physical pain right now?

    a. If so where in your body does it hurt the most?

25. Do you have a recent physical injury, or, have you had your pain for more than 6 months?

26. When did your pain start?

    a. Was there an emotional event happening in your life around that time?

    b. What was the emotional event that caused you pain?

27. Can you readily identify any other non-supportive programs you may currently have running?

28. Did you go and get a pad and pencil and write down the answers to these questions?

    a. If not, was it too much effort for you?

29. Can you see a pattern of this in-action in your life when it comes to finding solutions to your challenging issues?

30. Do you think you can change the beliefs you have right now?

The answers to these questions are the starting basics of 'Who' you think and feel that you are. If you were completely honest with yourself you should have had at least a few negative answers to the questions.

Now let's look at the answers you wrote down. What sort of language did you use?

In the What, Why and How questions study your answers. Did you use words like "I can't" or "I am"? If you did, these would be locked on beliefs of who you perceive you are and not likely true.

The challenge with any exercise like this is overcoming our inner fear of being emotionally honest with ourselves. It could take a few attempts before you allow yourself to honestly say what your inner voice is always telling you. There is no need for you to hide behind fear in this exercise. Nobody will see this information, only you.

The power of healing your self is in your ability to be honest with yourself, if not then you are likely to keep repeating the same mistakes over and over again.

All the beliefs and programs we are running affect us on physiological basis. For every thought there is a physical reaction within the body. In our next chapter we are going to help you create an understanding of how this process works.

Chapter Seven

How Emotions Affect our Health

We have taken you on quite a journey to this point in helping you understand Fear and how it affects your body on physiological basis.

Fear is at the root of our stress, our hatred for others and the things in the universe we do not currently understand. We Fear everything we do not understand and would sooner demonize it than logically take into consideration a new understanding and personal growth.

We still see this today in the wellness industry, many people would put down natural remedies as hocus pocus or some sort of voodoo and then go to a doctor and allow them to fill your body with toxic poisons that are at best only good for symptom relief and do not cure any of the challenges you may be experiencing.

Voltaire a French philosopher in the 1700's said, *"The art of medicine is to distract the patient long enough while the body heals itself"*

Nothing could be truer today than Voltaire's statement. The Hippocratic oath Doctors swore by years ago has become the hypocritical oath where-as many times doctors do more damage than good. I am not against doctors by any means I believe they serve a great purpose in the healing of people. That being said, there is a concern today that doctors are no longer following healing through the scientific proof placed before them but instead are held captive by the Darwinian Dogma that drug companies have all the answers to our illness. This fact has been proven incorrect time and time again through science and yet we still treat illness with drugs instead of more natural, less harmful remedies.

What Conventional Allopathic Medicine can and cannot do—If the provider and the patient had these kinds of clear distinctions in mind, it becomes possible to seek appropriate treatment and avoid wasting time, money, and effort on inappropriate treatment.

Allopathic Medicine CAN;

- Manage trauma better than any other system of medicine.
- Diagnose and treat many medical and surgical emergencies
- Treat acute bacterial infections with antibiotics
- Treat some parasite and fungal infections
- Replace damaged hips and knees
- Get results with cosmetic and reconstructive surgery

Allopathic Medicine CANNOT;

- Treat viral infections
- Cure most chronic degenerative diseases
- Effectively manage most kinds of mental illness
- Cure most forms of allergy or autoimmune disease
- Effectively manage psychosomatic illness
- Cure most forms of cancer
- Treat with Conventional hormone replacement therapies (too many side effects)(diet changes do work)
- Cure Chronic fatigue syndrome
- Cure Fibromyalgia or most arthritis'

When it comes to dealing with matters of the brain allopathic medicine has had a terrible reputation over the years; lobotomizing patients, psychotropic drugs which have deadly side effects, infirming patients who were not mentally challenged, etc . . . Today the DSM or

Diagnostic and Statistical Manual of Mental Disorders, has covered nearly every aspect of human psychological behavior with some sort of drug treatment. Most drugs are contrary to the manual in there healing nature boasting side effects of the drugs used as often being worse than the disorder in the first place. Every time I hear of a teen suicide or murder there is usually a youth involved that was being treated for depression or some other mental disorder with psychotropic drugs which had 'suicidal tendency' listed as one of its side effects.

There are less harmful ways to treat many mental disorders, but fear is not an unnatural disorder. You are not defective you are merely a victim of emotional circumstances and internal programs which have compounded over time.

No Thought lives in the body rent free

Every feeling thought we experience has a physiological effect on our body. In our workshops we guide people through a experiment called 'The Finger Rub Exercise'. The Finger Rub is an exercise in Kinesiology or also called Reflex Muscle Testing. Although the exercise is not an exacting science it does provide an interesting experiment in How your thoughts effect your body. Conditions which can hamper Reflex Muscle Testing are; time of day, toxins in your body, dehydration from not drinking enough water, or extremely stressed individuals. It is not an exacting science but proves to be a useful tool.

To perform The Finger Rub to yourself you simply follow the diagram and instructions below.

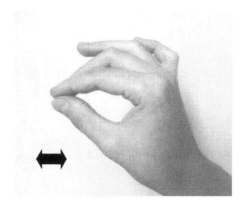

1) Begin by placing the pad of the index finger lightly on the pad of your thumb
2) Slowly rub the two fingers back and forth along their length
3) Make a true statement; "My name is _____" fill in your true name. The surface should feel smooth and slide with no friction.
4) Next make a false statement; "My name is Benjamin Franklin". The fingers will get sticky feeling or you will feel a noticeable resistance between the fingers.

If you felt the stickiness between the 2 fingers, then you just experienced a physiological response to telling a lie. *No thought lives in the body rent free.*

Now perform the experiment again steps 1 through 3. On step four think about a negative event which happened to you in your life or the last time you were angry with someone.

Did your fingers get sticky?

Once again, you experienced a physiological response to a memory.

To the brain and body these physiological reactions are happening with every thought you think. It is a stress response to a negative emotion in your body. In that very instant of your negativity every cell in your body reacts to some degree. At this moment the cells of your body are chemically changing states to either a state of growth or a state of protectionism.

In our office when we work with some clients we attach a stress thermometer to their finger and measure the differences in temperature at the finger tip when mentioning a particular event

or word. Temperature shifts of .1 (1/10th) degree can be noticed in seconds. We will use EFT to clear the emotions around the event or the word until there is no longer a temperature change. The Stress thermometer has become an effective tool in helping us determine the emotional relief thoroughness of our work with a client and is more reliable than the Kinesiology 'Finger Rub' exercise.

Can you physically see now why it is important that we learn to relieve these emotional events from our past and those feelings of fear and low self-worth?

When we consciously monitor our thoughts we become aware of our programs running and at that time we can choose to find a better feeling thought. It is in the seeking of the better feeling thought where we change programmed habits which have been running in us for many, many years.

In the study of my own emotions I was led to a philosophy which seemed to explain all the reasons my health had turned out so terribly wrong.

The book was 'Ask And It Is Given' –'The Teachings Of Abraham' by Esther and Jerry Hicks. It was my daughter-in-law who gave me a copy of this book as a gift one year. I could not put the book down it fascinated me so much and I felt like it was speaking a truth I had been seeking for my whole life. The book teaches of a consciousness which is tied to all things and every living cell in the body. Our emotional state is what guides the health of our body.

You are basically in two states, you are feeling positive emotions (growth cycle in the cells) or you are feeling negative emotions. How you feel determines the health of your body on a cellular level. You cannot wait until you feel better physically before you feel happier. You must strive for the better feeling thought now so that your body will follow with good intentions towards better health.

For all people it is hard to go from being depressed and feeling powerless to Joyful and Happy *(see chart on next page).* Those two emotions are at the extreme ends of the scale and feel like they are unattainable to reach so most people give up before even trying. However, there is some very good news; you only need to make a baby step on your emotional scale. Just moving from Depression to Unworthiness will give your emotional energy enough of a shift to have relief in the body. Think of it as taking a holiday from your stressful job. Your intention should be to slowly move up the scale of emotions with each shift the emotional relief gets better. After some time you will be in the healing healthy emotions which is where all miraculous cures of diseases lie.

There is no physical state in the body which cannot be changed using this emotional scale as a guideline.

All life is cyclical, just as the seasons change and day turns into night, emotions are up and down. The idea behind being consciously aware of your emotions is to keep them on the higher end of the scale and not fall victim to the deepest of negative emotions.

Our Fears drive our emotional scale into an unsupportive role. Over long periods of time of believing in our fears we will create physical ailments which match the emotions we are experiencing.

The Emotional Scale

Harmony	Growth	JOY/Knowledge/Empowerment/Freedom/Love/Appreciation
		Passion
		Enthusiasm/Eagerness/Happiness
		Optimism
		Hopefulness
		Contentment
Dis-ease	Protectionism	Boredom
		Pessimism
		Frustration/Irritation/Impatience
		Overwhelmed
		Disappointment
		Doubt
		Worry
		Blame
		Discouragement
		Anger
		Revenge
		Hatred/Rage
		Jealousy
		Insecurity/Guilt/Unworthiness
		Fear/Grief/Depression/Despair/Powerlessness

Chapter Eight

ONE SIMPLE TOOL TO ERADICATE FEAR FOREVER

Early in 2003 I ordered a financial program from a company. Due to the amount of money I spent on their programs the supplier gave me a bunch of bonus audio cd's as a gift. I spent a few weeks going through the cd library taking notes and performing the exercise when I came across this one audio cd by Paul & Layne Cutright. Called *'Freeing Yourself from Fear and Anger'*. The couple was very engaging and soft spoken as they taught, through this audio, how to use this new technique that had just been discovered in the mid 1990's for overcoming emotional challenges.

As I listened I thought, *"What kind of hocus pocus is this guy selling?"* My old programs of distrust and skepticism were rooted deep in me. However, I thought to myself, *"I will listen and instead of judging it right away, I will just suspend my disbelief for a moment."*

I listened as this man told the brief history of how this technique came to be. Mr. Cutright began by saying, *"This technique was derived from the 5000 year old art of Chinese acupuncture. It was based on an invisible energy system in the body that is not mapped by veins or arteries, muscles or nerve endings. It was discovered by a gentleman named Gary Craig and by tapping on these certain points on the body and saying a few words out loud the persons fear, anxiety, or pain would just simply go away".*

As I listened I am trying to figure out through this man's audio description of these tapping points, where on the body they were. First he had us rate our pain or fear on a scale of 1 to 10, ten being very painful and then had us write that number down.

He went on to explain more about the body's energy system and how it becomes blocked by negative thoughts. He then began this process of tapping and speaking. I followed along as best I could and repeated the words he said for a pain I had in my shoulder at the time. This pain in my shoulder had been with me for quite some time as I was a sufferer of chronic arthritis. It had never really gone away before this no matter what I tried. Even pain killers only mildly suppressed the pain throughout my body.

I followed along with the tapping and then after the technique was completed Mr. Cutright asked if anyone had any relief in what they were tapping on. Amazingly, I noticed the pain in my shoulder had gone down quite a bit. He did another round of tapping and again asked the question if anybody had a response in the audience he was in front of at the time of the recording. Once again I noticed my pain was nearly gone now. Mr. Cutright was doing this technique in front of an audience of nearly 700 people and with a show of hands he revealed they had over an 85% success rate in the audience.

I was amazed at my own results. Being the eternal question asker, I had to know more about this technique. I was able to contact Paul and I bought a few more of his programs. I then used this technique to deal with my pain but I only used it as symptom relief tool when my arthritis would flare up. Soon I was using it as a party trick when we went socializing with friends. They too had positive results and asked how the heck this thing worked so well. I believed at that point it was my cue to find out as much about this Emotional Freedom Technique as I could. I purchased more programs through the founder, Gary Craig's website. Hours upon hours of video DVD's filled my day as I watched and practiced along with the video's. I began to realize the true power and effectiveness of EFT as each week went by. I no longer suffered from Arthritis pain but even more I began addressing those negative emotional events that filled my early life. Those feelings of low self-worth began to melt away, my fears became irrelevant and I was becoming a happy person again for the first time since I lost my business 8 years earlier.

Life just seemed to be better. Of course people began to notice the change in me and when they would ask I would show them EFT. I was met with many raised eyebrows but the results were always there 100% of the time. As I taught this to other people I began to open awareness within myself. I could feel what the person across from me was feeling. I knew when they were lying about their emotions and I knew when I had hit a sore point in their life.

In the first few years when I began helping other people I used to have them tell the details of their emotional events but I found that hard on my own psyche due to the empathic connection I could form with the person. Imagine for a moment some person is telling you about the rape or sexual assault they went through and all the painful, hurtful feelings that are rushing through them are now rushing through you. It was overwhelming and I had to back away from helping people for a bit while I figured this thing out within myself.

I have never claimed to any psychic abilities, but I do believe we all have the power within us to intuitively feel another person's pain or pleasure it is part of the God Source consciousness which connects us all. If you remember for a moment you have probably felt that in someone else yourself. My challenge with these new attenuated feelings was, for so many years I had kept my emotions locked up and feeling that pain brought me back to the pain of my father's death and so many other deep emotions which I needed to fix in me. I see that early time of teaching EFT to others as my greatest teacher about myself.

I figured out that "I" was not a bad person after all. And, we all have these feelings at some point in our life where we question our own worth and value. I realized that I was part of something far more grand that is connected to all things through this thing we call the energy grid. My perspective and perception of the world, and us as individuals, changed to be more loving and forgiving of myself and everyone else. The truth is we spend so much time lying to ourselves about our feelings we truly miss the joy that each day can bring us. The joy of overcoming the false fears we have created about who we are and how we feel. It has been an empowering journey to knowledge and enlightenment that I would encourage anyone to take. As I shared this honestly with other people they too became aware of who they are and they too found enlightenment.

To date we have helped thousands of people worldwide through our workshops, Webinars, teleconferences, on-line self help videos and working one-on-one with so many wonderful people. And now, you will get to experience this self-empowering technique for yourself.

In the mid 1990's Gary Craig, an engineer, discovered by tapping on some key acupuncture points and saying a few words out loud, certain phobias seemed to vanish almost immediately. Gary developed and refined this technique and called it Emotional Freedom Technique. He spent many years performing workshops and refining his technique so that people everywhere could use this for nearly everything. Gary stated that it unlocked a blocked energy system in the body that would otherwise be flowing with health and wellness.

After years of using this technique on myself and others I have discovered my own understanding of how EFT works although I am still uncertain of the scientific reason behind the high success rate, I believe it is based around the focused healing emotions it lends to our consciousness during the phrasing of our vocal context of what we are working on. I will explain this more shortly.

In a scientific study done by *Dawson Church*, Ph.D., founder of the Soul Medicine Institute and author of *'Genie in your Genes'*, he discovered the process of EFT can actually lower Cortisol levels in the body by 25% and have a lasting effect for hours. As you discovered earlier in this book, Cortisol, can have destructive effects on our cellular make up when it is in high or chronic doses. By using EFT on a daily basis we could control daily stress in our lives and maintain our health without resorting to doctors and harmful medications.

Going beyond a daily routine of EFT we can also use it to neutralize the stress created by our very own fears, phobias and past emotionally traumatic events.

I do not believe EFT is a cure for anything, it is however, a very effective tool to use in lowering stress and relieving past emotionally traumatic events the result of which the body finds relief and heals itself. It is the discovery of loving yourself and in the relief where all emotional and physical healing begins. Just as we could use a rock to drive in a nail, using a hammer would be a more effective tool for doing that task and EFT is that tool by which this process can begin.

The first step in relieving a problem be that, pain, stress, fear or a traumatic emotional memory, is to first, emotionally, rate how strong this feeling is. To do that we use the Subjective Units of Distress Scale or SUDS as it is called.

To use the SUDS think of one particular thing you wish to work on and rate it on a scale of 1 to 10. Ten (10) being the pain or feeling is very intense. Write this number down. If you do not use the SUD scale to rate your pain or emotions it will be hard to tell how effective the EFT process will work for you. The reason behind this is, often times there may be a reduction in the pain or fear but not complete relief in your first few attempts. However, in witnessing some relief for yourself it may encourage you to keep going and find the seed of the condition you are suffering from.

One of the challenges I see today is, we all seem to be looking for 'The Miracle Pill' cure for everything and often times step over the remedies which actually work because we are consumed with focusing on the problem and not if there was any relief. ANY relief is good because it is the beginning to changing the negative emotional environment in which you have taught yourself to live. The cells in your body can begin the regenerative process and over a short period of time, conditions you once thought were incurable begin to vanish.

Using EFT one-on-one with a client I have never had to spend more than 25 minutes resolving even the deepest emotional trauma. Pain is usually relieved in 2 minutes and completely manageable within 10-15 minutes which is still faster than any pain killer on the market. The reason for the delay in complete pain management is the time it takes for your Endorphins, the body's natural pain killers, to relieve the pain.

In our workshops and lectures over the years we have seen miraculous results that would make even the skeptic see the power of this tool in resolving Fear, Stress and Pain challenges.

I can recall on more than one occasion a person in the audience who had suffered chronic pain for decades magically be completely pain free for the first time.

It all begins with the thoughts we are subconsciously feeling deep within ourselves.

EFT the technique that works:

STEP ONE—The SUDS check, <u>**do this exercise now**</u> for a pain or discomfort you are currently experiencing and write down your numbers which you are currently experiencing. We will use these numbers for our next exercise.

Next step of the Process is to teach you EFT.

EFT can be broke into 2 different sections, the 'Setup' and the 'Sequence'.

EFT—The Setup:

It is widely believed the Setup section of EFT, in short, turns your suggestive state on and opens the consciousness pathways in the body. I would add it may very well open the conscious pathways of the cells themselves as if a light were turned on and all cells were now paying attention to what is about to happen.

As I stated earlier, we have spent so much of our thinking time putting ourselves down or lying to ourselves about the feelings we are having. There is comfort in the very simple phrasing that perhaps for the first time we begin to believe we are of some value.

The Setup technique goes as follows;

While tapping on the 'Karate Chop Point' on one hand you repeat the following phrase three (3) times, ***"Even though I have this _____, I deeply and completely Love and Accept myself."***

The blank can be anything really. *"Even though I have this sharp Pain in my shoulder, I deeply and Completely love and Accept myself".*

Be as descriptive as you can with the pain or the specific emotion

Say this phrase 3 times and say it emphatically as though you truly believed what you were saying, even though many people have a challenge even whispering the words, *"I Love and Accept myself"*.

Here is where I feel a different kind of power lies with the process of EFT. Seeing now that we are emotional energetically charged communities of physical cells, you can imagine hearing supportive harmonious loving thoughts about yourself, it must be a first for a lot of you. We have spent most of our lives focusing on all the negative aspects of our life and never give consideration to the wonderful miracles of life we truly are. I have found we can also add to the Setup phrase by saying . . .", I deeply and completely Love, Accept and Forgive myself".

To me the most profound words of healing we can embody is, Love and Forgiveness, not for others but for ourselves. Learning to Love and Forgive yourself breaks down the base ingredients of Fear and withers their roots.

First we must start with finding acceptance, then find forgiveness for ourselves and finally feel love for ourselves. This is the healing juice you are looking for.

Psychologists have stated 70-80% of our thoughts are negative in nature, we experience a negative thought about ourselves every 11 seconds of our daily awake time. Imagine that of the nearly 80,000 thoughts we experience each day, nearly 60,000 of them are negative in nature. We are beating ourselves into submission with our own false beliefs and perceptions.

Perhaps this is the core of our cultural problem; if we are experiencing that many negative thoughts every day we truly must be out of harmony with 'who' we truly are. Perhaps we are creatures of love and compassion and have merely forgotten that part of us that is in alignment with everything good in the universe.

What if the world is a good place and we are living in a time that is perfect for our discovery of the old myths that we are something less than we were supposed to be. Wouldn't that be fantastic if you could discover this within yourself as so many of us have?

I heard a saying once, "There are only a few bad people in the world . . . they just move around a lot."

People are neither good nor bad, we are all just playing out the story of our belief's and perceptions of what we think is right. When we follow our cravings for something deemed sinful we believe we are a bad person. This is a false perception that lowers our self-worth and creates fear within us. You are not a bad person because you made choices or believed in certain ideologies throughout your life. Isn't it grand that we can change from who we are to what we want to become with the mere shifting of our thoughts.

Throughout my life I heard this saying, "You can't teach an old dog new tricks." When I heard this I would remind people that I am not an "Old Dog' but instead a human who has the ability to change if I choose.

The Sequence:

The Second part of EFT is performed by tapping on the following 8 points on the body and saying a 'Reminder Phrase'. It does not matter which side of the body you use or which finger or fingers you use to tap with. All that matters is get as close to the point as you feel you can and tap enough times (5-10) while you repeat the reminder phrase.

The Reminder Phrase is, *"This _____."*

For example; *"This Sharp pain in my shoulder"* or *"This fear of spiders".*

The points are as follows;

EB – Eyebrow – starting point after the Setup is complete is tapped at the inner edge of the eyebrow or just above where the nose meets the forehead on either side.	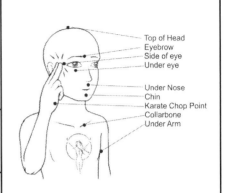
SE – Side of the Eye – This is the point at the outside edge of the eye socket on the bone	
UE – Under the Eye – directly below the pupil on the top of the cheekbone	
UN – Under the Nose – the point midway between the upper lip and the base of the nose	
CH – Chin Point – on the chin point between the lower lip and the curve of the chin itself	
CB – Collarbone point. – The point on the collarbone where it meets the breast plate.	
UA – Under the Arm – Under the arm, down from the armpit in line with the nipple line and midway between the front and back of your body	
TH – Top of Head – The crown of the head at its upper most point.	

Words hold different meanings for each person. Our minds do not think in words as much as it thinks in pictures. For example, if I say the word 'chair' you actually picture a chair in your mind. The same holds true if I were to mention the word 'father'. To me 'father' meant someone who was loving, yet stubborn. It is a fond memory and a wonderful picture of my father which instantly pops into my head. For someone else, 'father' could mean traumatic memories from their childhood and in an instant hearing the word brings back those faded memories and creates stress in the cells.

I could never guess what words hold meaning for you and what those meanings could possibly be. What I will do is give you a guide of phrases to follow and, as you say those words if a negative memory or feeling pops up, instantly, write that down, rate it using the SUDS check and work on that particular emotional memory.

Imagine for a moment, if a picture is worth a thousand words, then an emotional event can be a thousand pictures which in turn can relate back to one single word. It is how our mind holds memories and is called 'word association'. Through word association we are able to recall events from our life instantly. 'Word Association' is taught in some schools to help you remember and recall a persons name, dates or upcoming events. It ties the linked images in the mind to one word or phrase which creates instant recall from our memory banks.

To me the saying should read, "A word is worth a thousand pictures".

The emotions you feel around any word in your vocabulary dictate the positive or negative feeling thoughts you may encounter.

As we work with the 'Root Fears' perform the exercises regardless of the fact whether you think you may or may-not have that particular fear. What should be understood in this exercise is that you may have fears you do not remember, they may be unmarked or un-imaged emotions stored in your body from the emotional events and habits set in place within the womb or through the early learning childhood years.

Use the Emotional Scale *(Chapter Seven)* as guide to determine your emotional response to any given exercise we lay out for you. If they are negative in nature, rate them and work on those emotions.

EFT is very useful for clearing memories and fears even when you just use the Emotional Scale.

Unhealed Healers – On a study performed on 200 **health-care workers.** The breadth of conditions like anxiety and depression scores dropped by 40% and severity by 34% after just a few rounds of EFT. Pain dropped by 68% and cravings, such as for chocolate, cigarettes, alcohol, and drugs were reduced by 83%.

The Tapping Exercise:

Before we begin pick something, anything, that you currently have a negative emotional memory response or perhaps a pain in your body somewhere. Give the event a name, whatever comes to your head first.

Rate the Emotional event or pain on a scale of 1-10, ten being very emotionally charged or being in a great deal of pain. Write this number down.

Beginning with the Karate chop point start tapping and repeat these words out loud.

"Even though I have all these emotions around this _____ event in my life, I deeply and Completely accept myself" Repeat this line 3 times while continuing to tap on the Karate Chop Point.

If you are working on a pain say it this way. "Even though I have this pain in my _____ I deeply and completely accept myself" Repeat this line 3 times while continuing to tap on the Karate Chop Point.

Tap on the Eyebrow point and say, "All these emotions around this _____ event." OR, "All this pain in my _____." Repeat the same line, for now, while tapping on the remainder of the points; EB, SE, UE, UN, CH, CB, UA and TH.

Once you have completed this take a deep breath, let it out and Rate the event or pain again. Did your SUDS level go down even slightly?

Record this new number and repeat the exercise until you are down around a one or two on the SUDS.

Finding your Truth Exercise; (pg 90-95)

Now we are going to revisit the answers you gave on pages 90 through 95 and tap on those negative emotions you are experiencing in them.

For Example;

If on question one you answered no to; "Do you feel loved in your current relationships with your partner, family and friends?"

Then tap this in the following manner.

The Setup; "Even though I don't feel loved in my relationship with _____, I can deeply and completely Love and Accept myself." Repeat this 3 times.

The Sequence; While tapping on the remaining points simply say, "This feeling of not being loved in my relationship with _____."

The principle behind this exercise is to help you find peace in these emotions despite the fact that there is a possibility that you are not being loved by your partner, family or friends. You might think, "Then why do the exercises?" The answer to this is to help you come to an understanding that it is not your duty to get others to love you; it is your duty to begin loving and forgiving yourself. This is where all of your healing power lies. Finding peace in any given circumstance is finding your own self love within the event despite how you may have felt at the time.

In question 4 on page 109 we ask, "Do You love yourself?" This is a profound question that can be handled by asking "Why" you feel you are not worth loving.

In this example begin with the Setup phrase of, "Even Though I do not love myself, perhaps I can find Forgiveness and acceptance for who I am right now." While tapping on the Karate Chop Point, Repeat this line 3 times.

Now as we move in to the Sequence begin by tapping on the Eyebrow Point and tell the reasons why you do not Love yourself. Do not stop tapping until you have covered all the reasons, however as you finish the reasons use some positive ending phrases such as; "Despite my dislike of myself I can learn to Forgive myself.", "These negative thoughts are who I was not who I am." "I am learning to love and forgive myself"

These simple phrases have so much power on our psyche to change our inner emotional energy you will begin to feel better about yourself almost immediately.

When I was learning EFT and using it for my emotional life blueprint, I had lots of negative feelings towards myself. I can remember how much I used to loathe everything about myself; my looks, my character, my health. It all began to change as each day I would set aside a few minutes and just start tapping on all the negative emotions which were bottled up inside. One of the first things I noticed was that my physical pain went away and was staying away for longer periods. I began to receive comments from my friends and family like, "Do you ever look relaxed." It was true, I was moving away from that hateful state I was in for myself and most of the people around me to becoming more at peace within myself. I realized the people who used to upset me had not changed, I had merely changed the way I allowed them to affect me.

I am of the belief that negative people cannot drain our energy from us. What I have discovered is that we <u>allow</u> negative people to drain our energy from us. To give an example of this one of my favorite sayings is, "*You can take a lit candle into a dark room and light the whole room up. You cannot take a darkness candle into a room and remove the light.*" Have you ever noticed when you're at a gathering or party, how some people just light a room when they walk in and others can walk into the same room and go almost completely unnoticed? The unnoticed person is the darkness candle and they cannot bring everyone else down only the ones who allow them to.

However in saying that I will add this . . . Every thought we have has an emotional vibration a frequency if you will much like a tuning fork. As we gather others around us, they too have these thoughts vibrating within them. Now think of this as an orchestra each instrument bringing their own sound to the chorus. Somebody who is playing sour notes is easily recognized and it can change the sound of the orchestra.

As I worked on the dark aspect of my character I noticed that I began to be the person who shone brightly in the room with my relaxed nature and genuine smile on my face. What are you bringing to the party?

In Question 17 we asked; Do you blame others for the way you currently are? If so, How do you think they have affected you?

In the discovery of this statement you will begin to identify the hatred you have for yourself and closed minded you have become. Nobody is to blame for the way you are experiencing your life right now. We would like to blame others, however, I will guarantee you they are all situations which you have created and then use blame to cover up the fact that you need to work on yourself.

For this next exercise we will use the "Emotional Scale" from page 119 as a guide to clean up these deep rooted emotions we have.

There is no need to do a SUDS test on each emotion you only need to start with an emotional event and then find the emotions you are feeling around the event. For example; Pick an event where you may be feeling 'guilt' over what happened. Begin by tapping on the Karate Chop Point and say the following, "Even though I have all this Guilt around my _____ event, I can forgive myself for feeling that way." Repeat this 3 times while tapping.

Once again, moving on to the Sequence part of EFT begin with the emotions and then listen and follow your inner guidance to discover which other emotions you are also feeling around the event.

For Example;

EB – "All this guilt in my _____ event."
SE – "All this guilt for what I did."
UE – "All this guilt and anger"
UN – "All this anger at myself and at _____ for what they did to me."
CH – "All this anger and hatred towards _____."
CB – "How I hate that _____."
UA – "They Frustrated me so much."
TH – "I hope they get a taste of their own medicine."
EB – "I guess they are just playing out their games too."
SE – "Maybe they hate themselves too."
UE – "I still do not have to forgive them."
UN – "I can forgive myself for allowing myself to get involved with them."
CH – "I can forgive myself"
CB – "I can let go of this fear and move forward."
UA – "I am worth loving."
TH – "I can love and forgive myself"
Take a Deep Breath

In this example we just followed the feelings we had experienced through the event and we try and end on a positive note about our part or role in the event.

I have discovered in my working with other people as they come out of their depression and fearful state, the strongest emotion they begin to feel is rage and hatred for themselves and all the people involved in the emotional event. Understand this is part of the process as you move up the emotional scale. Allow those feelings of hatred to come forth and tap on them. Move yourself beyond the feeling until you are at the frustrated part before stopping.

Frequently Asked Questions

A few of the questions I am always asked when it comes to using EFT are;

1) *Do I have to keep saying the same thing over-and-over again?*

The answer is "No". As those thought-feelings are coming up deal with them and clear the emotions.

2) *Do I have to say everything out loud, it is a little embarrassing?*

This is a self-improvement technique that works best when you take some time in the beginning to work on yourself by yourself. After you have used EFT for a while on a daily basis you will notice you merely only have to think the thoughts when tapping and the emotions will clear anyway. So for now say them out loud.

And Finally the BIG question;

3) *What is the right phrase to use?*

The answer to this is that there is not a right phrase because words hold so many different meanings to each one of us.

If you are dealing with specific health conditions, I have found a great guide book to help you identify the emotional root of the physical condition is Louise Hays book(s) "Heal Your Body" or "Heal You Life".

In these books you can look up your particular condition and then associate the negative emotions which may have created the condition.

It is important to understand EFT is not a cure for anything it is a tool to be used to help your cellular body find relief. It is in the relief where your body begins the healing process. The older you are, the longer you may have been holding on to particular emotions. You need to understand that if it has taken you 30 years to develop a physical ailment because of the negative emotions you have carried; it may take some due diligence on your part to continually work on the emotions to disconnect the many different aspects of the emotional scale which you have attached to a particular emotional event and in turn reverse the condition. I will guarantee you this, if you are willing to put the effort in daily you will begin to notice healing over a very short period of time and complete disease reversal within 90 days.

The tendency is stop using EFT before we have resolved all the emotional aspects which need to be dealt with. Over 12 years of using this proven technique and working on myself and still today I tap every day. It only takes a few seconds and it feels good to feel good. Today I no longer work on past emotional events and the negative feelings I had for myself within the events but instead, I use it as part of a daily ritual for better health, the very same way I exercise every day, do deep breathing exercises every day and drink water every day. EFT has become a GOOD habit which benefits my health and as I see it the alternative to going back to the way I used to feel is NOT an option.

Using EFT on FEARs

To undo the fears and phobias we have formed our emotional habits around you need to only begin with the 'Seed' fears and work you way out to your current fear. Using EFT and a new understanding of the fear will resolve your fears and Phobias and give you everlasting Freedom from them.

As you are working on the fears using supportive finishing Sequence phrases like;

"It is OK to have this Fear of _____."
"I can feel safe now."
"I allow myself to feel safe and at peace with my fear of _____."
"I can forgive myself for feeling weak when it came to my fear of _____".
"I am strong in my heart and feel safe within."

I would suggest even if you 'Think' you do not have some of the particular fears listed in earlier chapters you work on them anyway. The reason behind this is we have developed a mechanism that protects us from being hurt by our fears. You will read more about this in Chapter 10—"You Can Be Right or You Can Be Happy".

As I have stated, EFT is a tool to help you clear the emotional trauma you have experienced in your life, it is not brainwashing just a gentle relief where those past images no longer haunt or hinder you.

Think of your life experiences as writing on a blackboard, EFT is the eraser we use to clear the writing from the board. There is however a latent image left in the background. The longer you have held on to your unsupportive beliefs the more you may have to use EFT to completely remove the latent image left behind from your experiences. I find using a combination of EFT for clearing the emotions and then using EFT with supportive affirmations has the best results.

Supportive statements while gently tapping on the points could be;

"I am learning to love myself"

"I am a good person"

"I have a loving heart"

"Inside of me lies all the answers"

"I am forgiving myself for what I thought was wrong."

These phrases ring through our body with a healing harmony. Each thought we have, speak and feel has a frequency much like a tuning fork. Loving supportive thoughts have been shown to vibrate much higher at a frequency that the mind and body need to heal.

Fear is the frequency at which self doubt resonates within us. Our true healing begins when we learn to love and forgive ourselves.

Phobia Relief Example—Fear of Flying;

When dealing with Phobias it is the same EFT technique. A phobia is merely an exaggeration of a base or root fear which has taken root and spread to another facet of your life. Although using EFT for the base and root fears will greatly lessen your phobia, sometimes it can be better dealt with by going direct to the phobia and speaking to it.

Following are a few examples of how to lower your fear for a particular phobia. This has been a favorite of mine when I travel because I usually meet up with people in an airport that are deathly afraid of flying. You can see the fear in their eyes so I usually approach them and ask how they are doing and eventually the conversation gets around to their fear of flight. I have even taught this to mothers with infants who are crying and overwhelmed by all the hustle and bustle around them. In the child example the wording changes but the results are the same. In this example we will only deal with 'you' the adult who may be experiencing this gripping fear.

First on a scale of 1 to 10 rate how much fear you have of getting on the plane. Next simply follow the EFT process with some of the following phrasing;

The Setup; *(tap on the Karate Chop Point of the Hand while repeating the following phrase)*

"Even though I have this Fear of Flying, I deeply and completely Love and Accept myself."
"Even though I have this Fear of Flying, I deeply and completely Love and Accept myself."
"Even though I have this Fear of Flying, perhaps I can overcome this challenge and Accept myself."

The Sequence; *(tap on the points as listed and say the phrase)*

Eyebrow point – "This fear of flying"
Side of the Eye – "My fear of flying"

Under the Eye – "This Fear of getting on that plane"
Under the Nose – "I am really afraid of flying"
On the Chin – "This fear of flying"
Collarbone Point – "All these Fears"
Collarbone Point – "All these Fears"
Under the Arm – "This fear of Flying"
Top of Head – "My fear of flying"

Take a slow deep breath in and let it out. Check your SUDS level and it should have come down.

If while you were tapping other aspects of the fear of flying came up, repeat the process using the new phrasing. For example, if is a claustrophobic fear of getting into the cabin of the plane, simply change the words to include, "That closed in feeling" and then rate your SUDS score again.

Phobia Relief Example—Fear of Public Speaking;

This phobia is one that I have received many calls on from people who were getting ready to go on stage and they felt overwhelmed and almost sick to their stomach over what was about to happen.

The phobia itself stems from the Fear of Being Judged, but remember, we ALL judge each other all the time. People will judge you whether you do something or not and believe me when I tell you most people do not focus on the mistakes you make in your presentation but rather on the content of your message. To overcome this phobia we will speak directly to the phobia and work the phrasing out from there. Once again give yourself a starting point on a scale of 1 to 10 how afraid are you of speaking in front of this crowd, now **write** that number down.

The Setup; *(tap on the Karate Chop Point of the Hand while repeating the following phrase)*

"Even though I have this Fear of speaking in public, I deeply and completely Love and Accept myself."
"Even though I have this Fear of Talking to all these people, I deeply and completely Love and Accept myself."
"Even though I am so afraid I will screw this up, perhaps I can just enjoy this process and Accept myself anyway."

The Sequence; *(tap on the points as listed and say the phrase)*

Eyebrow point – "This fear of public speaking"
Side of the Eye – "This fear of talking to these people"
Under the Eye – "I am afraid I will screw it up"
Under the Nose – "They are all judging me"
On the Chin – "This fear of Talking to these people"
Collarbone Point – "All these Fears"
Collarbone Point – "All my Fears"
Under the Arm – "This fear of Talking to these people"
Top of Head – "My fear of Public Speaking"

Take a slow deep breath in and let it out. Check your SUDS level and it should have come down.

Hopefully you are beginning to see that the patterns in phrasing do not matter so much as your honesty with yourself while saying the phrases. It is the tapping and your relief which changes the harmony within your body to become more relaxed around whichever phobia you may be talking too.

When you notice your SUDS level dropping on a topic, continue tapping until you are down to a 1 or 2, or the phobia does not to seem to matter anymore.

Now you have the tools and the opening understanding on how to use EFT and you have had a personal result with it. Of course we get much faster and deeper results in our workshops however, this is the method I used to overcome my fears and develop a new understanding of why I had my fears.

This is the most powerful tool I have ever seen for clearing fears and phobias. The same holds true for reducing physical pain and as you develop your skills 'You' will be able to tackle your emotional pain and find inner peace.

It is only a matter of using EFT daily and developing a new skill. The process itself is free, it only takes a minute or two and it truly is effective. You never have to reveal your life's embarrassing details to someone else who really does not care about your challenges unless they are capitalizing from you in some way.

Your past emotions will either Inspire you or expire you!

Coming up in our next chapter we will explore the condition of a virus in our bodies and our affect on our planet.

Chapter Nine

Our Body at War, Our World at War

We appear to be living in a time of hatred towards others; One Religion against a different religion; One Culture against another Culture; the 'Haves' against the 'Have-Not's'; who is Right and who is wrong.

In simpler times what mattered were family and community working in harmony. Today our perspective has been broadened to include the whole world as our 'New' community. The challenge is we are divided on who should have the right to rule or govern over all the communities of the world and our perception of their culture.

I listen closely as governments describe themselves as the savior who keeps us from total anarchy, chaos and being nothing more than blood thirsty thieves. The challenge with my perception of that belief is, it appears that it is government(s) and corporations which are creating the chaos in our world and murdering millions for their financial gain. The good of the people and their communities takes a much lower priority leaving private humanitarian organizations to take up the human cause and call attention to the atrocities being committed.

Every gun that is made, every warship launched, every rocket fired, signifies in the final sense a theft from those who hunger and are not fed, those who are cold and are not clothed.—Dwight D. Eisenhower

How will we ever find an order of governing to heal humanity and our planet?

There is a repetitive pattern in all things from the atoms which make up the molecules which make up our cells which make up the communities of cells which make up the body, the individual, the community, the cultures and so on. There are lessons on how to deal with this crisis in the cellular make up of our bodies.

I feel we could resolve all conflict in the world by understanding this delicate and just way our cellular body works.

Just a virus can pass through the body with no effect, we as humans can travel this world and visit other communities without conflict. Science has shown that all viruses and disease live within us at any given moment in time. However, it is not until the virus tries to invade the cells and become active where it will affect our health.

Like the viruses in our body when we meddle with the cultures we visit, we are looked upon as the virus is in their community and we open ourselves up to a repercussive outcome.

The same holds true in the militarization of the communities of the planet. During the first and second world wars the communities of the planet worked in harmony to eradicate what was commonly known as a common enemy. Nazi Germany was considered a Cancer of evil which needed to be eradicated. The Nazi's imposed their ideal belief of their superiority on the will of others and would stop at nothing less than domination over the countries within their reach and beyond. These actions triggered reactions from the opposing countries of the world who did not share Germany's ideology. Many countries were conquered and lie in devastation until the consciousness of the world became aware of this new threat to humanity and the preservation of the will of all the people. In reaction countries with entirely different ideologies were brought together to fight a common foe. I realize this is an over-simplified summation of the second world war but sometimes it is in the simplicity where we find our greatest of all answers.

Within the body the very same actions occur when a threat is detected that will compromise the well being of the body as a whole and the forces unite to conquer the perceived threat. Many of the body's normal growth functions are put on hold while the body's resources are spent on battling the invading virus.

Here is the challenge with our modern day culture as we live it right now; our governments and military forces are acting out as if they have the right to invade other communities and cultures for their resources. Just as this would not be allowed in the human body and its communities of cells, it creates only death and destruction in the other opposing community being invaded. The invader IS the virus not the supreme policing force we are led to believe they are. This is why those types of warring actions are never won and are always met with rebel forces trying to seek back their way of life. It also accounts for the retaliation we see happening around our world.

We have been coerced into believing that we are the ones who should hold dominion over all others. On any given day, at any given moment, you are being fed false propaganda to make you live in fear that someone is out to get your stuff, or steal your rights and way of living. The propaganda of the mind also plays out in our body as fear and stress and has an affect on our own well-being.

On one hand the military resources of the world were used to fight a common threat (the virus) for the good of all communities, on the other hand it is the common threat (rogue infection) to the community in which it invades and these battles can never be won. If collectively we could harness a new supportive belief throughout our world regarding these invading forces we would never have to see another war ever again.

If we were in harmony in our communities, being supportive and stimulating growth within, we would be the example by which other communities would find change. It is through our own harmony, love, compassion and growth that we best inspire others, within our cells, our bodies, our families, our social network, our communities, our towns, our county's, and our countries.

All communities of the world only want to grow and prosper, to be happy. Left alone this is attained. Meddled with it stirs up the anti-bodies which will fight the insurgence. The highest human value is cooperation, in our society today we falsely value competition over cooperation and compassion.

There are so many positive lessons we could learn if we only looked at the way our own cellular bodies react to any given circumstance. If we just pondered for a moment we, on this planet, are just communities of cells which make up a vital component of the whole of humankind. It is the diversity of cultures on this planet that makes us the wonderful humans that we can be. It is our diversity that makes us reach to become more in life. Allow other communities to find their growth and we will all benefit. When we rape our planet of its resources and oppress the weak we ARE the cancer and it is truly US that IS the problem.

We all have different beliefs and those beliefs should never be forced on each other. If your beliefs bring happiness and harmony within yourself then it is good for you. When your belief is destructive and forced on others then it is out of harmony with the common good of all. Beliefs should be able to be proven scientifically or at least held in regard for their merit and congruency.

No single ruler could ever hold dominion or rule over the collective unless there was a single consciousness for the good of all people on the planet and the planet itself. By creating a philosophy of every person having a purpose and a function within the community, we could nurture all life on our planet. We would also need to nurture every plant and the balance of nature to ensure our food sources are kept pure and healthy to feed the cells of our bodies. Our bodies were not designed to be fueled by toxins and deadly chemicals but instead living plant materials which it was designed to process into fuel.

We derived from the evolution and intelligent design of one cell and a singular all encompassing energy field. These single celled life forms through cooperation learned to band together to form new life and new living communities of organisms. These communities of cells evolved into us as humans and every other living thing on the planet. Imagine if we could learn to live within ourselves in harmony and within the community of humankind in harmony, what great things could we accomplish together. I wonder what level of evolutionary perfecting we could reach if we gave up this cancerous culture we have formed over so many years of our blatant ignorance of the simplicity of our universe.

Perhaps this will be relegated to being nothing more than a vision I have for humanity. The truth is within our bodies at all times there are rogue viruses waiting to find a weakness in the cells that they may capitalize from. Humanity will always follow this perfect design with rogue humans or communities seeking to exploit any weakness and gain control in some manner over the weaker of our kind. So the lesson should be that we find acceptance in that design and realize that without contrast we would never challenge ourselves to become more than what we are now. We would never learn to grow, just as the cells would not grow in a community that is no longer challenged with this perfect contrast.

Love, Compassion, Humanity, and Harmony are the keys to our survival as a human race.

I remember as a young boy a series of events which to this day confounds me how at such a young age I could be forever influenced by these few events which happened in another country. I can remember the mood in our home when I was only 5 years old at the news that John F Kennedy had been assassinated. The black & white images on the television flickered the replaying of that day over and over again. I can remember the sadness it caused my parents and how they spoke of this great man which had been taken away from us. At that time I did not understand governments, politics or even the geographical differences of other countries. All I was left with was this sense of great loss which I did not completely understand.

By the time I reached the age of 10 our conversations, as children, were being affected by a man named Martin Luther King. I can remember the feeling of hope he left inside of me as well as this new U.S. Senator called Robert Kennedy, or Bobby as he was being called.

These men spoke of peace, compassion for all human beings and cooperation. They filled our hearts with the feeling that the wars of the past would be forever gone and mankind would begin to live in harmony. I can remember my cousins and I playing and just feeling this hope building within us. Children do live care-free lives, for the most part, but this was different. The talk in the classroom at school had changed from historically looking at war to a new direction forward to the future where all good things could be possible for every person. We felt like all things were possible and cooperative harmony of all people was just around the corner. And then it happened, those unforgettable days in 1968 when the message of hope was squashed by two more assassinations. First, Dr. King and soon after Senator Robert Kennedy, our messengers of hope were cut down.

I can still feel the remorse that lingers in me for that time when all things seemed perfect. I did not understand at the time how these messengers of peace and harmony could be looked upon as the 'problem' and then be assassinated for spreading their belief throughout the world. The range of emotions, even for a young child, varied from grief, anger and revenge against those who could commit such a heinous crime.

I realize now there is no resolution in emotions of disharmony in the body just as there is no resolution for the challenges we face in our world today when we harbor these feelings of anger and revenge. I see now that when we hold on to this disharmony within ourselves we leave ourselves open to those elitists who will capitalize and use those feelings against us through their fear-mongering.

When we fall victim to any emotions of 'Dis-Ease' we leave ourselves open to the control of others over our lives. There is no harder crime against our own being than feeling we have the judgmental right over another's life to wish them ill will in any way. There is no resolution to be had.

As we take our lessons from cellular nature we discover that it is only through harmony and cooperation where we will discover our true healing power. As much as we have been taught to 'hate' and seek vengeance we must realize, we have been taught that way so that we can be controlled by someone else. These perceptions which have been handed down to us are false; we will never win the "War on Cancer" we will never win the wars of our world. In the body Cancer is reversed through nutrition and peaceful reflection. Our world can be healed the same way by making sure all humanity needs to be nourished and taught to find their inner peace no matter what their beliefs are as long as they are supportive of all humankind.

However, there is a large section of the majority of people who 'feel' this to be true and yet 'Think' the answers still lie in the old dogma of government and control. Today I find many people who feel we cannot do anything to change this outcome. "We have gone too far down the rabbit hole to change anything", they will say. Here is where an important point must be made, we do not need to change the world, we only need to change our view of ourselves within this world. Now that is an empowering thought. When you change yourself and let go of fear you actually change the world on a small scale. We are all connected through the energy consciousness and 'relief' in your self creates 'relief' in the energy consciousness. By simply sharing this simply philosophy with others the world can be changed and we are seeing this play out every day.

Today wars are being fought by less and less people who are willing to fight them at least this is what we are discovering in most civilized cultures around the world. People are beginning to realize that change can come through peaceful initiatives by banding together in communities to bring about change in our government and what we are doing to our planet.

This same scenario plays out within our body. By peacefully resolving our physical challenges through love and compassion within, the cells change within the whole of the body.

I look back at my years of chronic pain and illness and can see the anger I held inside. It was in the release of this anger where my body began to change. It did not happen overnight, but it did change over days, months and years. Culturally changing the world will be a bigger task, one that could take generations to bring about. In that change the planet will begin to heal, we will begin to heal culturally and perhaps our children and their children will witness the evidence of the power we have to heal ourselves internally and externally.

In our next chapter we going to look at the "Need to be Right" and help you find a new understanding of how limiting these thought are.

Chapter Ten

You Can Be Right Or You Can Be Happy!

There is need within us all to feel like we are right on any particular topic. If we look at conflict between two parties you will notice that one person feels the need to defend their position adamantly.

The need to be right.

There is no fear of being wrong, but there is a need to be right.

What could drive us so hard to close our minds and not listen to the opinions or facts that others present?

Why must we always face each debate as if it were a battle where there is only a winner and a loser? There is no middle ground from which to stand.

In negotiating any deal whether it is trade negotiations between countries, Land claim disputes between nations and first nation's peoples or workers wages there is this never ending conflict where someone must be right despite the facts that both people can win in any circumstance.

Without these different points of view we would have no contrast in our world and no need to grow and become more than what we currently are. However, it does not need to be done through conflict when instead change and growth can come from working towards the common good for all people involved.

When did we develop this Need to be right?!

In observing my father and his need to be right I noticed similarities that spans across all human beings. It begins with the 2 hemispheres of the brain and because emotional pain experienced in their life causes a false emotional state in the other hemisphere of the brain. To explain this more thoroughly we need to first look at the brain and listen to the language we use to describe ourselves. Then we will look at how emotions direct our thoughts into the false emotions of Pride and Ego.

On a daily basis we use both sides, Hemispheres, of our brain to process information in the conscious self and develop the thought patterns to write the programs in the subconscious self. However people can become predominantly more left brained or right brained thinkers.

| How thoughts are processed in the two brain hemispheres ||
Left	Right
The left brain hemisphere processes in a linear, sequential, logical manner. When you process on the left side, you use information piece by piece to solve a problem. When you read and listen, you look for the pieces so that you can draw logical conclusions.	If you process primarily on the right side of the brain, you use intuition. You may know the right answer to a problem but not be sure how you got it. You have a gut feeling as to which answers are correct, and you are usually right.
In writing, it is the left brain that pays attention to mechanics such as spelling, agreement, and punctuation.	The right side pays attention to coherence and meaning; that is, your right brain tells you it "feels" right.
Left brain people want to know the rules and follow them. If there are no rules for situations, they will probably make up rules to follow!	Right brain people are sometimes not aware that there is anything wrong. Think of it as a 'Polly-Anna' view of life where you see the good instead of the bad. The logical connection to action and reaction is not associated beyond the comprehension of the gut feeling.

When we consider the emotional scale you will discover there are emotional responses that are missing from the list. The key emotion which is the seed for 'the need to be right' is Pride. When we look at what Pride is we discover that it is what is known as a false emotion created out of the fear of pain. The emotional trauma created in the right side of the brain from past negative events creates the false emotion of pride in the Left side of the brain.

As we study this process see if you can make the connection of thought to feeling to thought functions happening.

Pride is an inwardly directed emotion that carries two common meanings.

The False Emotion of Pride

How the Pride process develops in the two brain hemispheres	
Left	**Right**
With a negative connotation, pride refers to an inflated sense of one's personal status or accomplishments. It could be considered a protection mechanism against the negative emotions experienced by the right hemisphere of the brain. Pride could also be defined as a disagreement with the emotional truth. Or a false sense of ones own excellence.	With a positive connotation, pride refers to a satisfied sense of attachment toward one's own or another's choices and actions, or toward a whole group of people, and is a product of praise, independent self-reflection, or a fulfilled feeling of belonging. The opposite of pride is either humility or guilt; the latter in particular being a sense of one's own failure in contrast to the notion of excellence.

All money means to me is a pride in accomplishment.
                                    —*Ray Kroc*

Anger is the enemy of non-violence and pride is a monster that swallows it up.
                                    —*Mahatma Gandhi*

According to Wikipedia:

> *Philosophers and social psychologists have noted that pride is a complex secondary emotion which requires the development of a sense of self and the mastery of relevant conceptual distinctions (e.g., that pride is distinct from happiness and joy) through language-based interaction with others.*
>
> *Pride is sometimes viewed as excessive or as a vice, sometimes as proper or as a virtue. While some philosophers such as Aristotle (and George Bernard Shaw) consider pride a profound virtue, most world religions consider it a sin, such as the Old Testament of the Bible used by Christians and Jews.*

Ego is the characteristic of thinking of one's self and the identity created of the self. Ego is not necessarily a bad thing to have as a matter-of-fact it is our desire for accomplishment and the creative discovery of becoming more that we expand and grow. However in the false emotion of Pride, ego is the consideration that we are already "better' than others and see no need in emotional growth.

We often think of the things that matter to us come from the heart. The heart feelings could be considered all the emotions of Emotional Scale we studied earlier in the book while Pride could be considered as the Left Brain thinking and False emotion of Pride and Ego.

Now back to my father, it is unfortunate that I did not know much about the life my father lived until after his death. He was a very reserved and stubborn man who never said much. He was not cruel by any means however he did not talk of feelings much and he did not show much emotion towards my siblings and me. We felt loved in our household but there was always this mystery around my father.

Years after his passing I began to ask questions about my fathers' behavior and began to discover just how emotional this man was. From early in his life as a small child he was forced to work hard for the family of homesteaders he was raised in. He was pulled from school after he finished grade 3 and became the patriarch of his family to help them make ends meet during the Great Depression years of the early 1930's. His job was to be the provider for the family so that his younger siblings could go off to school.

During the Second World War my father served as a medic on the front lines in Europe. He would never talk to us about his tour of duty during the war aside from this one conversation he shared when I was around 10 years of age. When I was growing up and attending school in the 1960's there was still a lot of chatter around the Second World War. One of my friends told me his dad was a sniper and that he had shot many of the enemy during his tour. He made war sound like it was glorious and noble, just like we saw in the Hollywood movies, and that he was doing a great service overseas. When I shared this story with my father and asked him to share his experience with me his response was, *"There is nothing glorious about war. It is only about death and destruction."* Today I can still hear his words but more so I remember the feeling of watching him turn inward to a place inside his mind where there was so much emotional pain. It was years later that my mother shared with us the emotional turmoil our father would go through with recurring dreams of the war. Today we identify this as Post Traumatic Stress Disorder, PTSD in war veterans, in those days however, you were considered weak if you could not handle it. Men were taught to disassociate their logical brain from the emotional brain. I see now that it was not because of sign of weakness but instead because of the pain of reliving the horrific trauma they endured during warring times.

The brain develops the false emotion of pride to separate the pain of the emotional trauma it has endured. To be wrong would be to consider opening the emotional prison which was built to protect us from emotional pain. When I see clients that have the strong urge to be right I realize that these people have endured great duress at an early age and have built this protectionism system which helps them cope with the emotions they have inside.

In my case, it began as a learned behavior from my father but then as life dealt its challenges to me, I found it a great coping mechanism to deal with all the weakness and emotionally charged events I had in life, one of which was the loss of my father at an early age.

You will remember from earlier chapters that the emotions experienced in the mind can manifest in to physiological conditions and disease in the body. Chronic emotional patterns create the 'learned helplessness' within in us which will make us give up hope.

When I used EFT to clear the trapped emotions I had inside my memories I felt no need to be right anymore. As a matter-of-fact it was quite the opposite; without the stress and duress I was able to think clearer logically and creatively to analyze a problem and find a common solution that suited both parties. The realization that all we think we may know is nothing more than a belief passed on to us from another source. The only things we truly know are those things we have experienced and learned to analyze through awakened thought and feeling.

Understand the 'Need to be Right' is not a persons need to be stubborn or a bully, it is their way of dealing with the emotional pain and fear they have inside. Once we take them through the process of relieving the emotions and fear the 'Need' disappears.

For ages, being 'wrong' has been associated with failure when in truth, being wrong should be celebrated as it is elevating us to a new level of understanding and awareness.

The Closing – Finding Your Truth

I have met many people who are too afraid to even try EFT on their fear because they are too afraid to open the emotional wounds they have inside. It can be a challenge to help them see that what they have in their life is directly connected to the fear they are holding on to. Often times these are the hardest people to change patterned habits in. We must take them by the hand and show them it is safe to follow the path of the feeling heart and that we will be right there for them.

Perhaps it is the spawn of our fears which developed into our false beliefs of how the universe works. Without our beliefs we would realize how worthless we may have perceived that we have become. We argue our point of view with such conviction that we feel malice and hatred towards those who would try and change that perception. It is the seed fear of pain, the emotional pain of being wrong, the emotional pain of being out of control, the emotional pain of others not liking us. For if we gave up our pride, who would we be?

When we look at the 'need to be right' it is so badly stained with pride and ego for one's self it can hardly be recognized from the fears which gave it birth.

Perhaps pride and ego are a defense mechanism from the fear of pain to filter its effect upon the host. Like amnesia to the patient who would want to forget the traumatic incident which nearly took their life or scared them beyond any thing they could ever have imagined before.

The question to ponder then becomes,: "Do we need to defend our beliefs over the beliefs of others at any cost?"

And, we must also look at the Darwinian Principles we were raised with as being false also. "The Origin of the Species" has become one of the most controversial books of all times. It is constantly relegated as the truth behind 'Evolution' and that in nature it is survival of the fittest that always wins. Our cultures have adopted the dogma of competition and our own superiority over the weak. This like any dogma (religion) has been falsely portrayed to us. In Darwin's book he only mentions "Survival of the Fittest" twice and yet he mentions the word 'love/cooperation', when talking about evolution, 98 times. I find it interesting that the man considered as the father of evolution spoke of evolving nature as one that happens through cooperation and harmony, the acts of love, more than anything else and yet we have created principles of competitiveness to better serve our society. The ebb and flow of creation, even at the cellular level, is one of cooperation first and competition lastly.

Nothing in nature takes more than it needs and when it does then it creates competition for resources and the destruction of the organism which fights for survival. All of nature is harmonious and balanced right from the animals and plants down to the cells within our bodies. Our FEAR of there not being enough to go around and our competition for resources will be our very downfall. Nature does not care if we as humans survive there will always be another creature which will rise from the ashes of our competition to once again work harmoniously with the elements of this planet.

It is OK to come into the light and not be afraid anymore. It is OK to not feel the need to be right. It is OK to be wrong or at least have a different point-of-view than what others may have. It is OK to question authority if their views do not reflect that of harmony and good for all.

Finding your TRUTH is finding something that resonates within you, it is a gut feeling. The challenge in the understanding is, what feels right to you may not feel right to someone else. Understand we are all looking for our own love and happiness, free of fear and being dominated. In that search we discover many clues from the truths of others and in those tidbits of information we discover our freedom in this physical life.

As we let go of Fear and replace it with understanding and a harmonious lifestyle, we are in congruency with nature that has evolved for hundreds of thousands of years from the single celled amoeba to the complex multi-celled creatures we have become. As long as we hold on to our false perceptions of fear and our need to be right we are left in a competitive state which is out of harmony with the whole of nature and the God-Source we were derived from.

I feel hope for you and for all humanity. My hope for you is that you realize there is nothing to fear but fear itself and you discover the truly powerful harmonious being that you are. It is no secret that you need to let go of all fear to find harmony within yourself.

In this book we have helped you identify fear and more importantly the seeds and roots of the fear you have that keep you from being the truly creative and wonderful person that you are.

Throughout the EFT exercises we have guided you through we have talked about the Subjective Units of Distress to help you nullify your Fear, Phobia, Pain or Stress. However EFT can be used to take you to much higher levels of happiness. All medical and psychological methodologies attempt to take the person from the negative state to a Zero point of either Pain or Emotional trauma. That is what all drugs are designed to do, to make the person basically feel nothing.

There is a new way of viewing our emotions that falls more in line with the Emotional Scale we have used in this book and it is called Subjective Units of Experience (SUE scale). What the SUE scale shows us is that we are not supposed to be in an emotional state where we feel nothing, we are here to experience life to the fullest and happiest we possibly can.

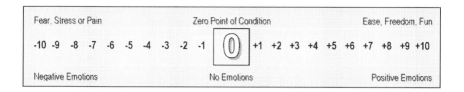

Fear, Stress or Pain										Zero Point of Condition										Ease, Freedom, Fun
-10	-9	-8	-7	-6	-5	-4	-3	-2	-1	0	+1	+2	+3	+4	+5	+6	+7	+8	+9	+10
Negative Emotions										No Emotions										Positive Emotions

It is not good enough to just get over something but to realize your potential to have so much more happiness. This is where all of nature thrives when we witness playful interaction. Watching the beasts in the field I see we are supposed to be so much more than what we are but have merely forgotten the playfulness we used to have inside.

Children spend much of their time at the higher end of the SUE scale playing, laughing and in a state of wonderment. As adults we have bought into the dogma that we are not supposed to be happy like children, we are only to feel nothing for true joy feels like something which is out of our grasp. Joy is something we left behind in our innocence but I ask you . . . Is that really true or is it just another false belief which we have developed?

You see I believe we hold the power to create the life we want for ourselves and it lies in those higher emotions of Joy, Love and Curiosity. The journey is well worth it as you leave behind your world of pain and fear. Now begin your journey towards feeling good it just takes practice. First practice feeling good, at ease, loved and very soon you will find these emotions will be validated by people and things coming into your life which will bring you more 'ease' and more 'love'.

I use EFT daily, not because I have "stuff" to work out but instead "Joyfulness" to discover. The "stuff' has been dealt with and it has been cleared but I have discovered there is yet another powerful use for this technique. The feeling is fantastic and the rewards are so much more than I could ever explain to you here on the pages of this book.

Use the EFT technique we gave you, daily, to lower your stress and raise those good feeling hormones your body needs to correct its physical and emotional challenges. EFT is the tool you have been looking for to help you correct the out-of-alignment feeling you have had for so long now and discover the happiness you thought could not be found.

If we are in your area, attend one of our workshops to witness the true power of self-empowered healing and a new beginning for your journey into fearlessness. The co-creative energy of a group of like minded people will elevate you to a new level of awareness and the love you have longed for deep within your heart.

Finally use the new philosophy you have discovered to become the person you are at the core of your being, the cooperative compassionate beings that we all are.

All change begins with one.

You are now the one that can change the world through the harmonious loving being that you are. As your consciousness raises, so does the consciousness of everyone around you.

If what has been said here resonates within you as feeling just then it more than likely is the truth you have been seeking in your life. It is the intention you came here to this physical plain to discover.

Have a Happier, Healthier, more Prosperous Life!

Thank You

Dan Brooks
Founder of GiveUpPain.com

For information on where and when you can attend one of our workshops contact us through our website at www.GiveUpPain.com.

Use this Promo code ___FearFree___ for a 10% discount off the retail price on any of our courses, workshops, G.U.P. products, or personal one-on-one guidance sessions with the author via telephone or in person.

email:

dan@giveuppain.com

Regular mail:

GiveUpPain.com
P.O. Box 66,
Port Loring, ON, Canada
P0H1Y0

Acknowledgements

I am so very grateful to all the mentors who have crossed my path through my life. Especially those who taught me how to think for myself, in this I honor my Mother and Father for their early lessons and for standing beside me, in spirit, to this day.

I Thank my older Brother and Sister for being such divine human beings and presenting me with such different philosophies. Believe me when I say, you guided me more than you can ever know and for that I am grateful.

To my wife Nancy, without your greatness, laughter and love of life I could have never realized my own worth. Thank you for seeing the best in me and for making me work on the worst in me. The contrast we endured gave me a vision to become a better man.

It is often said that wisdom comes from the mouths of babes. My four sons, Cory, Daniel, Nicholas and Brennan, have shown me what is truly important in life. The challenges and life experience you gave me helped me to realize the love and compassion in my heart. Your creativity and the true artists you are, have molded me to become the unique work of art that stands before you now. I am honored to be your father because you have all given me so much. The people you have brought through our house have shared their hearts and their traumas with us all and made us better people.

A special Thank You to my son Nicholas who has created the artwork within this book. When I asked Nicholas if he could create the cover art for this book I knew he would create a work of art.

We are the sum of the friends we keep and all my friends, old and new, have given me perspective and enlightenment. There are so many to Thank, that I could write a book on the blessings you have all given me.

A special Thank you to one of my prized pupils Nathalie for all you have become and are becoming, I salute you for the blessed artistic photographer and compassionate person that you are.

To my mentors who have guided me with their words and examples I am very grateful to you; Napoleon Hill, T. Harv Eker, Dawson Church, Brad Yates, Gary Craig, Jim Rohn, Robert Kiyosaki, Dr. Bruce Lipton, Louise Hay and a special Thank You to Esther & Jerry Hicks for the Teachings of Abraham.

And, to all the rest of you who I have crossed paths with in any form, you have changed me and been a blessing to me.

Other EFT guidebooks are available through our website;

**The ICUR's Method to Permanent Weight Loss.
The Balancing Act, Unveiling the Thin Person Trapped in the
Overweight Body**

This electronic book and guidance materials will help you overcome the emotional blockages that prevent you from achieving permanent weight loss. We take you step by step in the journey of learning the foods the body processes most effectively and will keep your body looking younger and feeling stronger.

About the Author

Dan Brooks is an Entrepreneur, Professional Trainer, Personal Performance Coach and the founder of GiveUpPain.com. He teaches from his experiences in resolving his own physical and emotional challenges which he has faced throughout his life. After over 17 years in Fire & Rescue Services, 3.5 years as a Paramedic and over 25 years as an Entrepreneur, Dan has gained vast insight into the human condition and has developed profound and effective methods of teaching and guidance to improve health, happiness and prosperity.

He is now a leading practitioner in EFT (Emotional Freedom Technique) and is often called upon by psychologists and emotional healing therapists for his unique guidance in helping people resolve life long issues.

"It was through resolving my own Chronic Pain and illness challenges that I discovered all emotional events, no matter how long ago they happened, can have an effect on our physical and mental health. There is a dogma throughout our healing therapies which does not teach fast effective natural methods to resolve emotional issues even though they have been scientifically proven to work. My objective is to guide, teach and self-empower people with knowledge and techniques that work and are life changing."

In the early years the techniques he discovered were taught in local workshops in Northern Canada and have expanded and evolved into world-wide tele-conferences and speaking engagements where thousands of people have found relief from their emotional limitations. All workshops and engagements are boasting an over 85% success rate in giving people tangible experienced results in less pain, less stress and less fear.

Dan believes that through inspired knowledge of the human body and the correlation to our own energy system we can begin a path of enlightenment and resolution to any physical or emotional challenge we face. It all begins with resolving the deep rooted fears we have internalized and succumb to which are giving us our current results.